*Form and Society
in Modern Literature*

Form and Society in Modern Literature

Thomas C. Foster

Northern Illinois University Press
Dekalb, Illinois / 1988

Library of Congress Cataloging-in-Publication Data
Foster, Thomas C.
  Form and society in modern literature

  Bibliography: p.
  Includes index.
  1. Literature, Modern-History and criticism.
2. Literary form. 3. Literature and society.
I. Title.
PN771.F64   1988   809'.93355   87–28311
ISBN 0–87580–134–X

© 1988 by Northern Illinois University Press
Published by the Northern Illinois University Press, DeKalb, Illinois 60115
Manufactured in the United States of America
Design by Anne Schedler

For my parents

Contents

Preface

This study grew out of a sense of frustration I felt when I first began to study Modernist literature seriously. I found that the habits and strategies of reading I had acquired in my earlier studies of Romantic and Victorian works availed me little, while the literary theories I turned to that were roughly contemporary with Modernism, specifically New Criticism and archetypal-mythic criticism, were little better. It seemed to me that the readings I was able to generate were incomplete; while they explained parts of the work very well, they stopped short of dealing with the whole of the works. And although Marxism provided a genuine alternative to those approaches, that alternative seemed to have a deeply ingrained and even constitutional hostility to Modernism. A great deal of commentary on Modernist works, and here *Ulysses* and *The Waste Land* are prime examples, has followed the tentative lines suggested by the writers themselves, and a great deal more has been a reaction against them, a retrenchment of earlier principles and methods in the face of novelty. So, the dilemma I found myself confronting, in general terms at least, seemed to me characteristic of criticism's relation to Modern literature.

Faulkner's *Go Down, Moses* is a case in point. When I first read that book, I was struck by a conviction that it was a novel—that it had unity and that it deserved attention as a whole—as one of Faulkner's best novels. For a long while, I labored to show that it was a single unit and that the essential structure of the narrative, from the whole novel down to individual sentences, was of a piece. I delivered a paper on the subject and began to feel pretty confident that I had accomplished my goal. Then another question occurred to me: having proved that the novel had unity, what had I said? The problem soon became less one of unity than of how I could understand that unity, that structure Faulkner elected to use, within the context about which he is writing. In a fairly short period of time, I found my whole approach to the question of poetic autonomy shifting. I had worked previously with the unstated assumption that I was studying self-contained objects with beginnings, middles, and ends, and that these objects, like Keats's urn, were oblivious to their surroundings. I now realized that my earlier assumptions were unsatisfactory, but I had not yet found anything with which to replace them.

Several things happened, more or less at once, to lead me to where I am now. I decided to take Wallace Stevens at his word when he says in "Of Modern Poetry" that poetry had to change because the world it confronted had changed. Another was that, while I rejected the Marxist notion that literature is somehow subservient to the socioeconomic structure of society, I found the concept of the literary work as process rather than product very useful. But the most important element in my progress toward a new position was that I kept reading Faulkner, and *Go Down, Moses* in particular. The more I read, the more I became convinced that the act of literary creation is a process of coming to terms with history, society, and literary history, and not simply a matter of producing well-wrought artifacts.

I then discovered that I had to bring my new principles of criticism, if they can be called that, to the Modernist works I wished to study and that I had to rethink my appraisals of existing critical theories as well. Moreover, my own confrontation with Modernist works led me to examine the attempts of other critics to define a Modernist movement or a Modernist aesthetic, and here I again found a surprise. I discovered that my original plan, to work up a definition of Modernism I could live with, no longer satisfied me, and it failed due to its very nature: defining a movement required the collection of specimens, the accumulation of objects, and, for me, a return to a discarded mode of thinking. I found instead that what really interested me was attempting to articulate a way of reading books and poems, not constructing a museum in which to keep them. What I also feared was the tendency of description to become prescription (as with Aristotle and the criticism of tragedy after him) and to become a principle of exclusion when it only means to define. Instead, I wished to develop a set of principles that would enable me to encounter the works not as further exhibits but as acts of confronting their culture.

What follows is the process of articulation, of discovering that set of principles, or at least a preliminary set, that will allow some initial soundings to be taken. There are a number of issues concerning Modernism that this study will not address; many of them deal with its literary history or its ancestry, its vital dates, or the list of authors or works admitted to the congregation. These issues, which I originally intended to examine and still find interesting and perplexing, are no longer immediately relevant to my purpose. I hope that what remains will not be unduly narrow.

I have employed the generic "he" throughout this study, although I have attempted to keep its use to a minimum. Personal taste and euphony militate against any of the combined "he-she" pronouns, which I find ghastly to read. My options, therefore, are limited to the male and female personal pronouns, and being male, I usually envision a male abstraction. I would certainly encourage women writers to use "she" instead, and I hope that my own decision in this matter excludes no one.

Form and Society
in Modern Literature

1 / Modernism, Criticism, and the Social Dimension of Literature

One of the more paradoxical aspects of literary history in the twentieth century is the way in which *modern* has become a term that applies not to contemporary literature but to a literature that is receding into the past. With the passing of time, the application of *Modernism* to the work of writers concerned with "making it new," in Ezra Pound's words, has changed the connotation from one of newness to one related to a specific moment in the past. This situation, itself absurd, leads to others even more so, such as the naming of the succeeding movement *Postmodernism*, which raises the question of how many prefixes the word will be able to stand (a game of names within names, appropriate enough for the Modernist sensibility). The modern paradox, then, is that in following what William Johnsen has called the "compulsion to be modern,"[1] the artist and critic-scholar have destroyed the term; in their act of being new, they have created an archaism.

This paradox is merely the first of many encountered by the student of Modern literature and, very probably, the least significant. At the same time, however, it serves as an anticipation of difficulties to be raised in attempting to define what Modernism is, or was; an accomplishment that has yet to be fully realized. Part of the reason for the failure of any completely satisfactory definition to appear is that literary definitions are inevitably false, through vagueness or exclusivity. Nevertheless, it is necessary to examine how others have described Modernism, in order to provide a starting place for further discussion.

Even the dates of Modernism are open to debate. To be sure, the twentieth century is marked with dates of tremendous global significance, including two world wars, and yet these dates seem to have little to do with developing or even defining the artistic sensibility of the period. The movement was already well underway and the major artists (except for the American novelists) already established before the first war, whereas the movement was virtually defunct by World War II and the artists, particularly the British, had for the most part died or drifted into silence. Despite this lack of temporal landmarks, there are general guidelines, if not specific agreements, concerning the Modern period. Monroe K. Spears sees 1870 as "marking a break from the past," although the specific period of Modernism begins for him in 1909, reaches its *anni mirabiles* in the years 1922–1925, and virtually ends by 1957.[2] Cyril Connolly believes the period slightly shorter, 1880 marking the "point at which the Modern Movement can be diagnosed" and 1950 ending the movement absolutely. Between those dates, 1910–1925 is the peak period, while at the end of the thirties "works like *Finnegans Wake* or Gide's *Journal* or *Between the Acts* resound like farewells or epitaphs. Yeats, Joyce, and Virginia Woolf are gone within six months of each other and everything the Movement stood for is dubbed degenerate art—or converted to propaganda."[3] The period of most general interest among critics is outlined roughly by these dates, and the works to be examined by this study all fall in the period between the wars, the two decades of "intensest" Modernist fervor.

Still other commentators, and some of the most frequently mentioned Postmodern writers among them, see twentieth-century literature as of a piece. John Barth has frequently protested that he cannot tell where Modernism leaves off and Postmodernism takes over, claiming that he does not know, therefore, in what camp he throws his tent. As evidence,

Barth cites a bewildering variety of categories into which his own writing has been shoved by critics. While William H. Gass may see differences between his own generation of writers and the Modernists, their similarities set off both groups from writers in earlier times. In *Habitations of the Word*, he contrasts modern writers with Fielding and Richardson, who

> require a fresh and interested eye, but the events themselves should intrigue it, the situations should excite. Joyce and Beckett and Barth and Borges expect a jaded eye, one already blackened by its most recent round in the ring, chary of further blows, not a bit innocent, for whom all the action, the incidents, the tension and suspense, are well known and over and dead and gone.[4]

Certainly perspective and intent have a great deal to do with how one defines modern literature, and Gass makes a strong case for those who wish to see that literature in the broadest terms.

Those who do not may feel more comfortable with Michael H. Levenson's *Genealogy of Modernism: A Study of English Literary Doctrine 1908–1922*. Levenson not only limits Modernism to fourteen years but narrows the scope similarly, so that he deems a very few writers Modernist: Lewis, Pound, Hulme, Ford, with Eliot and Joyce on the fringes.

If there is disagreement over the dates of Modernism, the arguments seem concurrent by comparison with various theories of what constitutes Modernist writing. The theorists cover the entire range of literary definitions from neo-Romanticism to anti-Romanticism, Naturalism, Classicism, Symbolism, and virtually any combination of these. There are, of course, agreements within the disputes, as well as disputes over the value or desirability of elements even within agreements over the elements themselves. Significantly, a preponderance of commentary has focused on the literary history of Modernism in trying to define it; that is, Modernism is an outgrowth of or a reaction to certain previous literary movements. That commentary should center its attention there holds several implications not only for understanding Modernism specifically, but literature generally, as well.

Perhaps the best place to start is with Maurice Beebe's postmortem, "What Modernism Was":

> First, Modernist literature is distinguished by its formalism. It insists on the importance of structure and design—the esthetic autonomy and the independent whatness of the work of art—almost to that degree summarized by the famous dictum that "a poem should not mean but be." Secondly, Modernism is characterized by an attitude of detachment and non-commitment which I would put under the general heading of "irony" in the sense of the term as used by the New Critics. Third, Modernist literature makes use of myth not in the way myth was used earlier, as a discipline for belief or a subject of interpretation, but as an arbitrary means of ordering art. And, finally, I would date the Age of Modernism from the time of the Impressionists because I think there is a clear line of development from Impressionism to reflexivism. Modernist art turns back upon itself and is largely concerned with its own creation and composition. The impressionists' insistence that the viewer is more important than the subject viewed leads ultimately to the solipsistic worlds-within-worlds of Modernist art and literature.[5]

Here, Beebe brings together several popular conceptions of Modernism, all of them growing out of the central notion that the artist is militantly antisocial in his act of creation. This notion is quite common among critics of Modernism; Edmund Wilson sees modern literature as a product of the willful separation from life, of Axel's castle.[6] Once he has removed the artist to the tower, the individual points he makes follow more or less logically. There are problems, however, with those considerations, as of course there are with any sweeping definitions, in that they either exclude too much of modern literature from Modernism if strictly applied or they are only partial.

For instance, his first point, that Modernism is distinguished by its formalism, is at once true and not very helpful. The Moderns are essentially formalistic, but Beebe does not make clear (perhaps it is not possible to do so) how much formalism is required of a writer before he may be considered a Modernist and whether or not he must, like Pound and Eliot, theorize about the form of his art, about the importance of the structure of his work, before being formalistic. If, by formalism, Beebe means that writers consciously reject prescribed forms (metrical lines and regular stanzas in poetry, authorial intervention, consistent chapter development, beginning–complication–climax–denouement structure in the novel) as requirements of art in favor of a constant struggling after forms that will satisfy the demands each new work places on the writer, then his assertion seems valid enough. At the same time, however, the rejection of the style and form of one generation by another is scarcely restricted to this century; Wordsworth's rejection of eighteenth-century poetics in favor of a purer "form" is but one recent example from earlier literary history.

This argument is not entirely unfair to Beebe, for it points up a major problem in Modernist criticism: that while structure, design, and style—formalism—are integral parts of Modernist literature, no one seems to be able to point to a specific use of any one feature and say, "This is the characteristic Modernist use of structure." The argument does not suggest, of course, that there is a single structure common to all Modern writing. So far, however, few critics have dealt with Modernist formalism with the depth that many have shown in dealing with Modernist themes. While the problem exists within all genres, it is particularly apparent in the case of fiction, for which there is a wealth of information on the uses of structure and style in various individual works but comparatively little of a general nature that is useful. Nor should the situation be surprising; it is very difficult to enumerate similarities among Joyce, Lawrence, Hemingway, Faulkner, Woolf, Fitzgerald, Forster, and Ford, to name just a few who must be considered, once we have noted that all employ justified right margins in their printed forms. There has been more general discussion of the characteristic form of modern poetry, but there, too, it is difficult to find uses of form common to not only Pound and Eliot, but Yeats, Frost, Lawrence, Stevens, and Tate.

Beebe's other points suffer from similar difficulties. As he points out himself, irony is scarcely confined to this century. The Augustans are probably more detached and ironic than the Moderns, although it may be that the kinds of irony are not the same. Similarly, reflexivism, art's concern with its own creation, predates even Impressionism by at least a few hundred years, occurring, among other places, in Milton's early poetry and Shakespeare's sonnets. Reflexivism well may be more representative of Modernism as a whole than of any other movement or period. However, two points really are tied up in this one, and it might be valuable to separate the two. Art's concern with its own production and worlds-within-worlds do not seem precisely the same. For instance, the novel's concern with itself is evident in *A Portrait of the Artist as a Young Man*, while *A Passage to India* does not manifest the same trait, and yet both are concerned with worlds-within-worlds psychological interest that nearly everyone acknowledges as distinctly Modernistic. Reflexivism seems more a point within the larger point than a characteristic in its own right. It certainly exists, but the question is whether it is a universal quality. Then, too, it must be remembered that Beebe first published these remarks in "Ulysses and the Age of Modernism," so that, understandably, his comments are tempered by his work with Joyce.

Beebe's treatment of Modernism is vocally anti-Romantic. He claims that the movement developed autonomously, without aid from earlier literary periods, although he is willing to credit Impressionism for passing reflexivism along to the Moderns. He also recognizes that his views stand in direct opposition to those of many other critics who believe Modernism to have developed directly from Romantic tradition. Cyril Connolly goes even further, to assert that Modernist literature is a culmination of the best traits of more than one previous movement:

> The modern Movement began as a revolt against the bourgeois in France, the Victorians in England, and puritanism and materialism in America. The modern spirit was a combination of certain intellectual qualities inherited from the Enlighten-

ment: lucidity, irony, scepticism, intellectual curiosity, combined with the passionate intensity and enhanced sensibility of the Romantics, their rebellion and sense of technical experiment, their awareness of living in a tragic age.[7]

Connolly's remarks are unfortunately brief, coming as they do in a short introduction to a list of what he considers the one hundred best books of Modernism, for it would be interesting to watch him resolve the apparent paradox of irony on the one hand and passionate intensity on the other. Furthermore, irony as used by the Moderns is less a matter of scepticism than of detachment, there being a modest though significant difference between the two. Indeed, Joyce's ideal artist paring his fingernails hardly seems a model of passionate intensity, although perhaps Joyce the writer living solely for his art does.

Robert Langbaum, who expresses a similar theory, sees a major difference between the modern Romantics and their nineteenth-century counterparts:

> Our best writers . . . are twentieth-century romanticists who have managed to sustain the potency of the self by joining it to powerful outside forces—by recognizing, for example, that the self is not, as the nineteenth-century romanticists tended to think, opposed to culture, but that the self is a cultural achievement, that it is as much outside us as inside, and that the self exists outside us in the form of cultural symbols. In assimilating ourselves, therefore, to these symbols or roles or archetypes, we do not lose the self but find it. When writers are as deliberate and self-conscious as this, however, in bridging the gap between the individual and the culture that seemed to make tragedy impossible, the art they come out with may have or suggest the richness, depth, and complexity of tragedy, but it must be in its final effect comic or rather tragicomic. That is why tragicomedy would seem to be the characteristically modern style in literature.[8]

While the premise that the best modern writers are romanticists is not very useful, the main idea of recognition and self-conscious usage of the archetypal existence of the self is. The writer who comes after Freud, Jung, and Nietzsche is able to see the archetypal possibilities of myths, that our myths are implicit in our very existence, and therefore can dismiss those myths as religious–spiritual guides and use them structurally, selecting, modifying, mixing myths from various cultures and epochs, to order his art. This is the same point that the professed anti-Romantic, Beebe, addressed. Whether tragicomedy is the characteristic literary style of Modernism is another matter entirely. Inasmuch as an ironic literature precludes high tragedy, even in a tragic age, tragicomedy may well be the prevalent mode of this century, although Joyce's jocoseriousness seems closer to the mark. Langbaum's contention that our century is incapable of high tragedy is expressed by other critics as well, notably by Raymond Williams in his study, *Modern Tragedy*.[9]

Still, Langbaum's most interesting insights remain in the field of myth and archetype:

> The psychological interest passes over into the mythical at that psychological depth where we desire to repeat mythical patterns. Life at its intensest is repetition. Mann tells us that the ego of antiquity became conscious of itself by taking on the identity of a hero or god and walking in his footsteps.[10]

He raises two important points in this passage. The first is that life at its intensest is repetition, and the second is that twentieth-century literature probes the psychological depths at which mythical patterns exert their influences. This great depth, in its turn, leads back to an older god, one that Nietzsche dredges up in *The Birth of Tragedy from the Spirit of Music*[11] and that Monroe Spears applies specifically to Modernist literature in *Dionysus and the City:*

> He appears to the Greeks not as a magnified but familiar human form thrown on the clouds, like the Olympian deities, but as more mysterious and disturbing. Against the Apollonian tradition dominant in Socrates, Plato, and Aristotle, with its emphasis on the normal and rational, the cultivation of the aristocratic self-sufficient individual, the criterion of sanity and health, he represents the claims of the collective, the ir-

rational and emotional and abnormal; of the feminine or androgynous or perverse; of intoxication and possession, surrender to non-human forces; even of disease. Hence, once more he is a fitting embodiment of the modern concern with these matters, from Conrad's *Heart of Darkness* (1899) and Mann's *Death in Venice* (1911) on through Forster's *Passage to India* (1925) and many other avatars to the recrudescence beginning in the latter 1950's.[12]

Dionysus is for Spears the rather obvious link between the twentieth century and earlier Romanticism, but at the same time, the god goes beyond that linking function to embody dark, mysterious forces that Spears views as characteristic of modern literature. Certainly, the claims of the collective can be seen as a twentieth-century concern, particularly in light of modern interest in the mythic and archetypal; in the individual, private self's relationship to the cultural, universal self; in the rather disturbing power seen in the masses, especially non-European masses. Faulkner's Benjy would be a foremost instance of the interest in the irrational or abnormal, in direct contrast to the previous century's many voices of reason and intelligence. Indeed, it is precisely on the basis of Modernism's apparent infatuation with the abnormal that Lukács bases his attack on its lack of perspective. He sees evidence in the creations of Musil, Kafka, Joyce, as well as Faulkner, that the modern, naturalistic (as he sees it to be) novel fails to live up to its responsibilities to its community, to create lasting human types, to recognize aberrant individuals for what they really are. It is precisely this Dionysian element of modern fiction that he attacks, the Apollonian that he valorizes. His selection of one type over another, Thomas Mann over Franz Kafka, demonstrates the failure of Spear's assessment of Modernism as Dionysiac literature to encompass the entire range of Modernist works.[13]

The Dionysian interpretation works extremely well for those Modernists who exhibit strong romantic ties, such as Yeats and Lawrence, and for certain works or parts of works by other writers as well. At the same time, however, it seems that Spears may be entirely mistaken in dismissing the Apollonian influence too summarily. Beebe, for one, strenuously objects both to Spears's insistence on Dionysus as the god of the age and to the general idea that Modernism is essentially Romantic:

> If we see modern poetry as a current which moves from Whitman to Frost to Graves to Ginsberg (to Bob Dylan?) and if we see Lawrence, Hesse, Hemingway, and Mailer as the major novelists of the twentieth century, then I suppose it may be possible to see Modernism as only another wave in the incoming tide of Romanticism. But what then do we do with Flaubert, James, Conrad, Ford, Woolf, Forster, Shaw, Pound, Stein . . . and James Joyce? To label these writers Romantic seems to me a clear case of mistaken or insufficient identification, and to reduce them to the status of minor writers would violate all sense of critical justice. Monroe Spears says that "if any god personifies modernism, it is Dionysus," but try to imagine Henry James on a Dionysiac frolic with Virginia Woolf and Thomas Mann. Surely a stronger case could be made for the major Modernists as Apollonian.[14]

Beebe's first point rings true; few names on the list he offers (the proportions of which in the original were truly staggering) can really be called Romantics. His hypothetical "frolic" is indeed more than a little difficult to image, and it serves both to lighten the tone of the debate and to point up Spears's vagueness. Spears, however, is not talking about a rollicking, jovial god of wine when he speaks of Dionysus, but rather a darker, mysterious, almost unknowable force. Among the writers Beebe mentions, nearly all make use of some aspects of what Spears labels the Dionysian, at least occasionally. Nevertheless, neither label—and here Beebe falls into the same pit he digs for Spears—neither *Dionysian* nor *Apollonian* really satisfies as a term to describe the entire range of Modernist literary interests and treatments. And here is the problem with not only the labels at stake in this particular debate but with literary labels in general: they are either too restrictive to fit properly, or they are constructed so loosely as to be meaningless.[15]

The problem of labels is particularly troublesome in the

ongoing argument over the literary heritage of Modernism, since to identify one literary period or movement in terms of another doubles the problems of definition and abstraction. Having said, with Wilson, that Modernism is a continuation of Symbolism; with Langbaum, of Romanticism; with Lukacs, of Naturalism; with Graham Hough, that it is a detour from the main tradition altogether;[16] even with Harold Bloom, that it is the inheritor of an inheritor of an inheritor, each weaker than the one from which it inherits;[17] what have we really discovered about the nature of any particular Modernist work? Very little, it seems to me. The best the process of labelling can hope to achieve is identifying parts of the whole, elements within the larger body. Any label that attempts to embrace the whole of Modern writing is doomed to failure by the shortness of its reach.

The other peril lies at the opposite end of definition: one may become so inclusive as to be largely meaningless. Ihab Hassan, in his marvelously entertaining *Paracriticisms: Seven Speculations of the Times* lists what he calls seven rubrics of Modernism: (a) Urbanism, (b) Technologism, (c) Dehumanization (Elitism, Irony, Abstraction), (d) Primitivism, (e) Eroticism, (f) Antinomianism, and (g) Experimentalism. These seven categories are extremely difficult to reconcile with one another. How, for instance, does Dehumanization square with Eroticism, Technologism with Primitivism? Even here, however, the qualities he points out are not universally valid. One may rightly point out that those Modernists who carried the banner at Vanderbilt University—Tate, Ransom, Warren—were not only not urbanists, their platform rested on a foundation of agrarianism. Of course, Hassan seeks in this definition not so much to describe Modernism in its own terms but to show how it was a passageway to Postmodernism.[18] Indeed, Hassan's chief interest in discussing modern literature is to arrive at a discussion of *Finnegans Wake*, which he identifies as "creating peculiarly postmodern forms": "Parodic Reflexiveness," "The Re-Creation of Reality," "Nonlinear Forms," and what he calls "the Problematics of the Book."[19]

Jerome Klinkowitz argues a similar line, particularly in *The*

Self-Apparent Word: Fiction as Language/Language as Fiction, when he aligns modern writers like Joyce and Stein with Postmodernists like Beckett and Burroughs in striving to move beyond self-effacing literary language to what he calls self-apparency.[20] Modernism, however, stopped short of real self-apparency, since it appeals to groundings outside language itself (as in the case of the schema of *Ulysses*, with its emphasis on body parts, Homeric parallels, and art forms) and therefore still is partly self-effacing.

Still others, such as James Mellard in *The Exploded Form: The Modernist Novel in America*, seek to erase the modernist–postmodernist distinction altogether, replacing it with a view of all of twentieth-century literature as of a piece. Mellard breaks the movement into three sections, calling them "naive," "critical," and "sophisticated" Modernism. While Mellard's views are provocative and intriguing, his names for the three modes point to a danger implicit in dividing up modern literature: nearly any system of categories, of necessity, carries with it loaded labels.

The problem with these various definitions is not that they are not true; quite the contrary, they all quite accurately describe aspects of Modernism. Unfortunately, like the fable of the seven blind men describing the elephant, their truths are limited and in turn provide only limited utility to the student of Modernism. Levenson notes that modern writers were perfectly capable of harboring conflicting ideas. At one point, he argues that the movement was "individualist before it was anti-individualist, anti-traditional before it was traditional, inclined to anarchism before it was inclined to authoritarianism."[21] His study offers convincing evidence to refute the more simplistic position of those like Bernard Bergonzi or Fredric Jameson who claim for Modernism a straightforward elitism or authoritarianism and who metonymically identify modern writers with the fascism of Pound or Lewis. Later, Levenson notes that Modernism moved simultaneously toward two extremes: "radical egoism and similarly extreme formalism."[22] To identify the movement along only one of those axes, then, is necessarily to falsify its nature.

Therefore, we must look for another way of understanding

Modernism: if not the ancestry of the movement, then perhaps the process of creation. Spears supplies a starting point, when he states that free verse and rhetorical discontinuity are no longer satisfactory criteria for defining modern poetry, and then looks for suitable defining ideas or movements:

> Perhaps the largest generalization that can be made is that there are two primary impulses in modern literature, both always present but one or the other dominating. The first is the drive toward aestheticism, toward the purification of form, its refinement and exploration, the development of those features that are most distinctive. The illusion becomes more convincing and self-sufficient; there is a tendency for the art-world to become more separate and independent from life. This is countered by the opposing impulse, to break through art, destroy any possibility of escape to illusion, to insist that the immediate experience is the most important thing. . . . The drive toward form and then through it, to art and then beyond it and back again to reality, truth, immediate experience, and the incorporation of this whole process into art— these are central to modernism.[23]

This passage illustrates a problem common to virtually all critics of modern literature: how to reconcile the obviously formalist impulse present in so many Modernists, particularly the impulse to talk about the importance of form, with its absence among the many others who rarely discuss it. Spear's explanation helps to reconcile in part the apparently irreconcilable, although it does not really go far enough. He applies his theory to the movement as a whole, saying that some people are formalists, others "life-ists," but as Johnsen shows, this same idea of motion back and forth between life and formalist aesthetic can be carried a good deal further:

> Newly sensitized to the Modern's own mistrust of myth and metaphor, we find allowing for individual permutation, Moderns such as James Joyce, W. B. Yeats, T. S. Eliot, and D. H. Lawrence articulating a common, three-fold pattern of experience: (1) Man suffers the frustrating disparity between a fallen outer world of disorder and a more perfect inner world,

he exchanges the soft, wet outer world of disorder, contingency and chaos for the hard, dry inner world of metaphor, myth and history.

(2) Man realizes both the falsification of reality that order inevitably produces, and his loss of immediate contact with humans and things; confronted with a world becoming ethereal and narcissistic, he returns to re-examine the real, the natural, the unordered.

(3) Facing again two polarized choices, man tries to envision an excluded middle when he comes to realize what the structuralists understand: opposed choices are inverted mirror images of each other, mutually dependent, ordered by a common point of view. Existing between polarities, the excluded middle or third possibility cannot be grasped with the same sureness as the first two stages.[24]

Johnsen's dialectic of modern literary creation encompasses and puts into perspective several contradictions or disputes that show up in the work of other critics. When the work is seen not as an object with qualities but as a process of negotiation and relationship, it becomes possible to understand that the work may contain both the Romantic and the anti-Romantic, the Dionysian and the Apollonian, the formalistic and the anti-formalistic within the same structure. The false or incomplete labels for qualities can then be seen for what they are, identification of elements of a larger process rather than complete explanations. Moreover, the process can be taken a step further; what Johnsen describes is a movement witnessed primarily on the level of character or persona, while the dialectic encounter of self and world can be said to happen on all the levels of creation. The form of the work can be understood as a social and historical as well as artistic act, by which the writer makes a response to his society as well as his specific artistic situation, for the two cannot finally be separated. Such an understanding holds the possibility of understanding the Modern work whether it be essentially formalist or not, whatever one's understanding of that term may be, as of a kind with other Modern works by virtue of its relationship to its society and to literature.

If one defines Modernism as a characteristic action or process rather than a characteristic product, then one can begin to overcome certain misunderstandings based on the appearance of the poem or the novel or whatever. This enhanced understanding can lead, in turn, to a conception of Modernism that genuinely advances our understanding of the specific work at hand. Moreover, the concept of process can lead to a further understanding of those initial difficulties in facing the Modern work itself and of trying to define the movement more generally. If literature is a total historical process—that is, if it is a movement within and through history, society, and culture as well as other literature—then we are not free of Modernism but instead still are living through it. However absolute the midcentury rift between Modern and Postmodern may appear, the one is tied inextricably to the other.

Before turning from these discussions of Modernism to the literature itself, I should like to examine some major developments in critical theory over the last half-century in terms of two related considerations. First, where do these theories locate the literary work in its milieu; and second, what implications does that placement have for the Modernist works with which we are concerned? There are a number of reasons for pursuing this limited objective, not the least of which is spatial. Moreover, the placement of the literary work would seem central to a critical theory, as a point most likely to reveal underlying biases and ideologies as well as the point from which readings of individual works emanate and judgments about broader categories, such as the nature of literature, become possible. Thus, even in its truncated form, such an examination is essential to an understanding of how critics approach Modernist literature.

There are three general ways in which the literary work has been understood by criticism over the last fifty years or so. The first two grow out of an understanding similar to T. S. Eliot's in "Tradition and the Individual Talent":

> The existing monuments form an ideal order among them-
> selves, which is modified by the introduction of the new (the
> really new) work of art among them. The existing order is
> complete before the new work arrives; for order to persist after
> the supervention of novelty, the whole existing order must be,
> if ever so slightly, altered . . .[25]

The first school of criticism employs the notion of literary
works as monuments, as completed objects, and has gone
under the loose appellation *New Criticism*, although the term
Anglo-American (to distinguish it from the Russian cousin to
Structuralism) *Formalism* is preferable, since it is more descriptive of the primary concern of so much of the criticism
practiced by Ransom, Blackmur, Burke, Tate, Richards, Emp-
son, and Brooks and their colleagues and followers. The second type of criticism goes beyond the notion of monuments
in isolation to a position more closely approximating Eliot's
ideal order; the literary work, however radical it may be, becomes a moment in literary history, a continuation of, or reaction to, or variation on the existing body of literature. This
category encompasses not only Eliot and his followers, such
as Northrop Frye, but also critics such as Harold Bloom who
seek to demystify the notion of an ideal order and therefore
are nominally at odds with Eliot, as well as a great deal of
generic criticism from E. D. Hirsch to some of the Structuralists.

The third major critical mode involves the privileging of
some other discipline over literature, so that the literary work
becomes a sociological, or economic, or psychological, or linguistic artifact. The privileged discipline, usually one of the
social sciences, subsumes art into itself, lends its terminology,
often its method as well, to the critic, who then plays the
results back into the master discipline. Stated so schemati-
cally, this sounds tautological—ask an economic question
and you get an economic answer—but behind each of these
various methods is the need, usually unstated, to see literature in terms of a context larger than itself. In other words,
the works of literature do not form an ideal order among
themselves, or if they do, that order is subordinate to a larger

order. Where these theories create difficulties is in the implication carried by the notion of subordination, that literature is a secondary and derivative activity.

The problem at the outset, then, is this: how can literature maintain its identity as a distinct activity without falling into that separation suggested by its modern apologists? By way of addressing this issue, it will be necessary to examine the positions held by proponents of these three modes of criticism, and then to suggest a method of mediating among them, of studying the form of a literary work within its cultural context.

———————

In *The New Criticism*, John Crowe Ransom attacks the ethical emphasis of Yvor Winters' poetics:

> Now I suppose he would not disparage the integrity of a science like mathematics, or physics, by saying that it offers discourse whose intention is some sort of moral perfectionism. It is motivated by an interest in mathematics, or in physics. But if mathematics is for mathematical interest, why is not poetry for poetic interest.[26]

And elsewhere he characterizes Winters thus:

> Mr. Yvor Winters is a victim of the moralistic illusion, but independently of that comes closer than anybody else I know to realizing what I should regard as the most fundamental pattern of criticism: criticism of the structural properties of poetry.[27]

These two statements portray fairly accurately the salient points of theoretical American Formalism (as opposed to its practical workings, which sometimes differ a great deal). The impulse behind such a stand originates, I believe, from the reactions against two essentially Victorian ideas still holding sway in the academy (and elsewhere) at the time of the New Critics' ascension to faculty positions. The first is the notion of a utilitarian art, that literature can be used to accomplish social goals, and the second is the study and teaching of literature as a philological–historical procedure, a literary analogue to Darwinian scientific study. The vehemence with which some of the formalists reject these older practices is largely a response to the ferocity of the attacks by scholars of the old school against criticism.[28] The result of these reactions is to produce a theory in which poetry becomes an insular object, cut off from other aspects of experience. In the first of the Ransom quotations just cited, for instance, Ransom evidently takes *poetic* as a synonym for *aesthetic* in his attempt to sever poetry from ethical concerns after the fashion of the sciences. While elsewhere he does not deny that poems have meaning, that meaning nevertheless is intrapoetic, closed off from the world outside the poem.

Another formalist who follows Ransom in his insistence on insularity and who is even more programmatic in establishing his theories is Cleanth Brooks. A poem for Brooks is a linguistic object, a closed system. He further reinforces that closure by his split between referential and emotive language. By eliminating the referential side of language from poetics and relegating it to the abstract, denotative, exclusive language of the sciences and seeing poetic language as emotive, concrete, inclusive, and paradoxical, he eliminates the possibility, theoretically at least, of the sort of demands Winters makes on poetry.[29]

Moreover, he further solidifies that position by his "heresy of paraphrase," in which he claims any statement about poetry is an abstraction from it; that is to say, the critic is reduced to using referential language to discuss the emotive language of the poem itself. His statement, therefore, will necessarily be limited and thin in comparison with the richly dramatic presentation of the poem itself. This position is at once one of Brooks's chief contributions to criticism and a major liability in his own critical position. It is a positive contribution inasmuch as it removes the possibility of a reductionist, utilitarian criticism whose main criterion for judging poetry is whether the message serves society well. The liability for Brooks himself lies in the problem of following his own precepts, as Kenneth Burke points out regarding his study of Faulkner.[30] In practice, it will be nearly impossible and, I believe, not even desirable to wholly avoid the thematic elements of literature, since however emotive the language of a poem may be, it must still refer in some degree to the world outside itself or readers could never understand it. Brooks himself recognizes this problem:

> [The poet] must return to us the unity of the experience itself as man knows it in his own experience. The poem, if it be a true poem is a simulacrum of reality—in this sense, at least, it is an "imitation"—by being an experience rather than any mere statement about experience or any mere abstraction from experience. (Urn, 213)

Brooks is sufficiently aware of the flaw in his discussions of poetry that he must remind the reader that he knows it exists; at another point, however, he says that critical practices and attitudes of the past force him to take what is essentially a weakened position to successfully combat those practices and attitudes. But the "simulacrum of reality" statement muddies the flow of his thought a good bit. Throughout *The Well Wrought Urn,* he insists that poetry is a special mode of language, that its use of language is what distinguishes it from the sciences. Then, at the end of the text, he slips in the notion that poetry is also a matter of recreating reality or some imitation of it. This basic inconsistency in his position is what Burke counterattacks in his examination of Brooks's study of Faulkner. Brooks himself apparently fails to recognize how much that contradiction compromises his theory.

This split in his thinking is constantly present in the book and manifests itself most clearly in the tension between his theory and his practical criticism. Nowhere is the tension more explicit than in his discussion of Yeats's "Among School Children." Here, he incessantly moves outside the poem to the poet's life, his mythological system, and the history of ideas, although he nevertheless steadfastly maintains the impropriety of doing so:

> But I believe that, in making such an interpretation, they have allowed themselves to be too much influenced by the assump-

tion that the woman in Yeats's thought must be Maude Gonne; and have therefore concluded, from the dates of the poem— the perils of biographical bias!—that the Ledean body is that of an old woman. (Urn, 183)

The perils he alludes to in this passage are not so much those of biographical bias as of shoddy reading that relies too heavily on biography. The context of the Ledean reference would seem to exclude the possibility that, whatever Maude Gonne's age at the time of the poem, the poet is dreaming of an old woman's body. At the same time, there is no need to attack, as Brooks does here, the propriety of biographical information in criticism, particularly not when he has just employed information from outside the poem:

In Yeats's system of symbols, man and woman are related as the two cones in his figure of the double cone—one waxing as the other wanes, waning as the other waxes—in dynamic antithesis. The sphere, by contrast, is a type of harmony and repose. The blinding of nature which they experienced went beyond sexual attraction and repulsion: it was a childlike unity of being. (Urn, 181–182)

Given the statements he makes elsewhere, Brooks's introduction of outside material at this point is indeed curious, since of all the references in the poem to the material of *A Vision*, this one perhaps is damaged least by ignorance of that material. Certainly, the richness of the passage is diminished by such a spare reading, yet it seems possible that a reader could enjoy and understand this poem with no understanding of *A Vision*. Brooks violates his precepts at a moment when, seemingly, he need not do so.

That he does points to a confusion in his theory, made clear in the closing paragraph of the chapter, in applying the dancer–dance metaphor to the poem itself:

It is entirely legitimate to inquire into the dancer's history, and such an inquiry is certainly interesting for its own sake, and may be of value for our understanding of the dance. But we cannot question her as dancer without stopping the dance or waiting until the dance has been completed. And in so far as our interest is in poetry, the dance must be primary for us. We cannot afford to neglect it; no amount of notes on the personal history of the dancer will prove to be a substitute for it; and even our knowledge of the dancer qua dancer will depend on some measure on it . . . (Urn, 191)

The confusion of this passage resides in Brooks's ambivalence toward the dancer's history—literary biography—as an element of criticism and perhaps, in part as well, from a misunderstanding of the Yeatsian question that forms the central metaphor of this passage. The position he argues against, rightly, suggests that literary biography can successfully substitute for genuine criticism of the literary work. That such approaches not only existed when Brooks formulated this argument but are with us still is attested to by the work of critics who seize the poem as an opportunity to psychoanalyze the poet. Brooks stumbles on just what the role of biographical information should be: having excluded it on one level, he cannot seem to articulate the terms of its reentry or its significance. Moreover, the metaphor breaks down in his statement that we cannot question the dancer during the dance, for while ceasing our reading in midpoem to search for illuminating data could hardly be considered a satisfactory method, we can take a knowledge of the poet into our reading that can inform our understanding of the poem as we read. Brooks's model of the reading process, as demonstrated in this passage and elsewhere in the book, suggests a single-minded rapture on the part of the reader that experience will not bear out.[31]

Because the poem is constructed with words, the reader is constantly pushing into areas beyond it to search out meanings that enrich his appreciation of that poem, unlike the viewer of the dance, whose appreciation of the dance is relatively passive. The division between intrinsic and extrinsic meanings dissolves precisely because words imply, suggest, extend beyond themselves. This is true of even the least poetic, most neutral sorts of prose; one of the great contributions to language studies by the Marxists has been their demonstrations of the ideologies and prejudices betrayed inadvertently by writers whose intentions were to convey logic, reason, and equilibrium. In poetry, where the intention often is to be more inclusive, the distinction breaks down even further, and with it Brooks's dancer analogy. Again, it is useful to remember that he is forced in part into the extremity of his insistence on always looking inward at the poem, toward its core, because he is reacting against a criticism that stands almost wholly outside the work itself.

Extremity is a useful word to bring to the discussion of Brooks at this point, for it may be objected, justifiably, that he represents not the norm of American Formalism but its furthest limits. Certainly his fellow New Critics have tried to distance themselves from him:

> The worst difficulty with Brooks's method, as we see it in operation, is this: that any poem in which he can detect the ironical or paradoxical structure—and he can detect it almost anywhere—appears to him excellent, and nothing except this structure appears, in his opinion, to be involved in the art of poetry.[32]

Winters goes on to object to the method of *The Well Wrought Urn* chiefly because of its lack of ethical or judgmental (the two are often synonymous) grounds. Yet, it is in connection with Winters himself that Ransom suggests a critic like Brooks as the model New Critic, several years prior to the appearance of the Urn, by his attack on Winters' moralism as inappropriate to criticism and his subsequent praise of the structural analyses themselves (when separated from the moralism).[33] Similarly, Burke's disagreement with Brooks has less to do with Formalist theory than with individual practical permutations. Therefore, while Brooks stands at a far edge of Formalism, he is nevertheless representative of the movement generally, for his extremity lies not in departures from orthodoxy but in his programmatic insistence on that orthodoxy.

An implicit feature of the Formalist method, if not of all its critics, is its bias toward the Modern poem. The structure of

The Well Wrought Urn, as it runs from Shakespeare and Donne to Yeats, tacitly maintains that all poems can be subjected to the same method, that, as Winters complains, there is no basis for value judgments in this criticism. The chief beneficiary of such a position is the new poem, which must no longer wait for its writer to die and be valorized, reviled, or emulated by subsequent writers in order to find its way into the academy, but which now becomes legitimate material for criticism the instant it is published. Allen Tate notes this phenomenon of the New Critics' work and sees it as a mixed blessing:

> A modern poem becomes history for the fewer before the few, a handful of unprofessional readers, can read it, or read it long enough to dry the ink. Our critics, since Mr. Richards started them off with *The Principles of Literary Criticism* in 1924, have been perfecting an apparatus for "explicating" poems (not a bad thing to do), innocent of the permanently larger ends of criticism. They give us not only a "close reading" but the history of the sources of a new poem by Eliot or Stevens . . . before it is able to walk. Within five years of the appearance of *Four Quartets,* we knew more about the poem than Mr. Eliot knew . . .[34]

The Formalist method invites, by its very nature, the kind of instantaneous attention to the new poem of which Tate speaks, which benefits not only the living poet by lending legitimacy to his creation but also the critic, for whom a completely new field of study opens up. What Tate sees as a liability in this practice is the lack of time for separating fad and judgment, a tendency in the valorization of the new to valorize simply because it is new. Tate, in asking that the poem be allowed to learn to walk, asks for time enough for sober judgment to overtake the worship of novelty. Of course, there is no way of building such safeguards into a "pure" Formalism, just as there is no way of assuring discernment and skill in the critics who practice it. The New Criticism, however much it may be based on older poetry, lends strong support to the new poem, and in its tacit connection of old and new, it moves toward the second part of Eliot's "monuments" statement, toward the notion of an ideal order or literary continuum.

Many of the critical theories that have succeeded the New Criticism have viewed the literary work in ways related to, or growing out of, Eliot's ideal order of monuments. In so doing, they have cast aside a Formalism based on the organic unity of the individual work in favor of a formal typology. By substituting the system of literature for the work of literature as the basis for study, they have exchanged one notion of poetic autonomy for another. Among the proponents of such theories, Northrop Frye stands out as one of the earliest and most persistent, as well as perhaps the most influential. Other critics working from similar (although by no means the same) starting points are E. D. Hirsch, with his genres or types; Harold Bloom, with his theory of poetic misprision; and Geoffrey Hartman, who in *Beyond Formalism* aims at very much the sort of shift away from New Critical Formalism that we are discussing. Frye, of course, offers the clearest connection to Eliot, in his statement that *Anatomy of Criticism* is an attempt to annotate the concept of an ideal order.[35] Bloom also suggests the notion of a body of literature in such statements as "Poems rise not so much in response to a present time, as even Rilke thought, but in response to other poems,"[36] although he introduces a tension between the new work and the preexisting order altogether missing from Frye.

What *Anatomy of Criticism* purports to do is raise criticism to the level of a science, or a social science, that can proceed systematically and impartially through the literary field and that is now nonexistent:

> If criticism could ever be conceived as a coherent and systematic study, the elementary principles of which could be explained to any intelligent nineteen-year-old, then, from this point of view of such a conception, no critic now knows the first thing about criticism. What critics now have is a mystery–

religion without a gospel, and they are initiates who can communicate, or quarrel, only with one another. (AC, 14)

Such a statement suggests that a major factor in making criticism scientific is the tyranny of the university; if it won't teach, it isn't valid. It further suggests that coherence and systematization are the most important elements in developing such a science, and indeed, the heavily schematic nature of the *Anatomy* bears out this latter suggestion: Frye's impulse toward pattern elaboration and taxonomic classification frequently leads him to steamroll the individuality of the single work. His concept of science, in fact, is closest to nineteenth-century biological taxonomies:

> If criticism exists, it must be an examination of literature in terms of a conceptual framework derivable from an inductive survey of the field. . . . The presence of science in any subject changes its character from the casual to the causal, from the random and intuitive to the systematic, as well as safeguarding the integrity of that subject from external invasions. (AC, 7)

By criticism, then, Frye means a classificatory activity, a placing of works within a "conceptual framework," within a larger literary context than the works themselves. He accomplishes this placement by "stepping back" from the work (AC, 140), by moving away from it where the New Critic presses closer.

Despite this methodological difference, however, he shares with the New Critic a notion of poetic autonomy, and in fact, he is as explicit as Brooks on the point when he says, in *Fables of Identity*, that the critic deals with the literary work by freezing it, ignoring its movement in time, and examining it as a completed and, by extension, self-contained pattern of words.[37] However, he pushes this reification even further and actually suggests a commodity–consumer relationship between poems and their readers, particularly in the Polemical Introduction to *Anatomy of Criticism*. His rhetoric is consistent, from his image of the critic as middleman or consumer's researcher (AC, 20) to his statement that the critic should move toward the "undiscriminating catholicity" of Wilde's auctioneer, equally appreciative of all literature (AC, 25).

That he conceives of literature as a product to be consumed, an autonomous object, further betrays itself in the heavily noun-oriented manner of his criticism:

> For some reason it has not been nearly so well understood that discursive writing is not thinking, but a direct verbal imitation of thought; that any poem with an idea in it is a secondary imitation of thought, and hence deals with representative or typical thought: that is, with forms of thought rather than specific propositions. (FI, 238–239)

Frye's radical disjuncture of the acts of writing and thinking, in the first part of the passage, carries two major problems. The first is something like the problem of representational art in classical thought: in the present instance, art, or writing, can never be more than an imitation of thought and stands at a remove from the genuine intellectual activity of thinking. Writing, then, becomes a necessary parasite, the transmitting form for a preexistent content. The question that follows from this position runs something like this: If writing is a secondary mental activity, in what way does it obtain its value? For Frye, of course, the value of literature lies everywhere except in what he would describe as its idea–content. Such a bias, however, brings us to the second problem, the essentially static nature not only of art but of thought as well. Thought, in this context, can be brought into being without language, in a state of pure mind. It is only thought—not the process of thinking but the final product—with which writing can deal. Writing, speech, language has no shaping function: thought occurs at a prelinguistic level of mind, and language's job is to body forth a suitable imitation. Such a conception denies the possibility that language and thought are related more closely, that writing is not merely the form to thinking's content, but that it plays a decisive role in the thinking process, that thinking in any prelinguistic state is incomplete at best, that there is no content without form, nor for that matter, form without content. The second part of the passage mainly is a development of the first: the poem, since it is more concerned with form than is discursive writing, is even less able to deal with ideas. This position is particularly telling, since the poetry in connection with which these comments are made, Wallace Stevens', is so heavily idea-laden. Moreover, the relation between poetry and idea is not only often specific, but frequently quite active as well, particularly in a poem like "The Man on the Dump," which is not only a representation of an idea (the poet as man on the dump) but is the act of the poet wading his way through the refuse of poetry, beating out his own dissonances on "an old tin can, lard pail." Stevens consistently gives us not the static representational forms Frye suggests but poetry, actively encountering world, idea, and itself, "The poem of the mind in the act of finding / What will suffice."[38]

Even so, Frye must necessarily reduce the work to its forms, for his object of study is much wider than that of Brooks. The individual work is rarely of much interest to Frye, qua individual, although it is a necessity as a point of departure for his criticism. Indeed, his metaphor for relation of critic to work is one of distance, of standing back:

> In looking at a picture, we may stand close to it and analyze the details of brushwork and palette knife. This corresponds roughly to the rhetorical analyses of the new critics in literature. At a little distance back, the design comes into clearer view, and we study rather the content represented . . . The further back we go, the more conscious we are of the organizing design. At a great distance from, say, a Madonna, we can see nothing but the archetype of the Madonna, a large centripetal blue mass with a contrasting point of interest at its center. (AC, 140)

The rhetoric here is telling: at a great distance, that is to say the distance from the piece at which he elects to work, everything except the archetypal pattern is obliterated—we can see nothing but, he says—and the individuality of the work is lost. This loss, however, is not a restriction but a liberation from the restrictions of the New Critical attachment to the work; he is freed, in short, from the tyranny of the poem, so that he may examine poetry.

And, indeed, the procedures he follows in his practical criticism bear out this theoretical bias toward the general. In the already-mentioned essay on Stevens, he forsakes discussion of any of Stevens' poems in favor of Stevens' poetics: using snippets, lines, and overtones from the *Collected Poems* and an occasional passage from *The Necessary Angel*, Frye attempts to demonstrate the ways in which Stevens is "one of our small handful of essential poets." Nowhere in the essay does any one poem receive more than passing attention. More commonly, though, his method moves him outside the writer in question altogether, into the larger category of literature:

> We said that we could get a whole liberal education by picking up one conventional poem, Lycidas, for example, and following its archetypes through literature. Thus the center of the literary universe is whatever poem we happen to be reading. One step further, and the poem appears as a microcosm of all literature, an individual manifestation of the total order of words. (AC, 121)

Again, he is the victim of a rhetorical betrayal. What he evidently wishes to suggest is that the individual work interests us because it distills the archetypes into a single, special phenomenon; whereas, what in fact he conveys by the phrase *"whatever* poem we *happen* to be reading" is that the individual poem is of interest only insofar as it dissolves itself and allows us to observe the larger patterns working through it.

Here again, his biology metaphor is the ruling principle: the individual is of interest only as a representative of its type.

> That such patterns exist leads him to his theory of a literary universe: the study of archetypes is the study of literary symbols as parts of a whole. If there are such things as archetypes at all, then, we have to take yet another step, and conceive the possibility of a self-contained literary universe. (AC, 118)

> All poetry, then, proceeds as though all poetic images were
> contained within a single universal body. (AC, 125)

The step he proposes in the first quotation is a short one.
Archetypes must have a source of power; and if one rejects
the Jungian collective unconscious, as Frye does, then the
source must have a material location, the total collection of
written words: literature. The movement of poetry, then, is
inevitably backwards, toward the source. The tension in the
individual work is not one of breaking with or overcoming
previous literature, as it is in Bloom, but one of joining with
it, of becoming part of a community, and thereby escaping
the ignominy of total individuality. And despite his methodological differences, Bloom surely must have a similar notion
of a "total order of words" behind such statements as

> Let us give up the failed enterprise of seeking to "understand"
> any single poem as an entity in itself. Let us pursue instead
> the quest of learning to read any poem as its poet's deliberate
> misinterpretation, as a poet, of a precursor poem or of poetry
> in general. (AI, 43)

or

> . . . we are dealing with primal words, but antithetical mean-
> ings, and an ephebe's best interpretations may well be of
> poems he has never read. (AI, 70)

The only way we can possibly make sense of the second of
these passages (since Bloom never explains himself) is to see
behind it to a concept of a literary universe, of "poetry in
general." The first passage, too, sounds like Frye in its premises (although it moves in different directions), in its demand
that we stand back from the individual poem so that we may
see a larger context.

Such a concept of an autonomous literary universe leads
to difficulties for both critics, difficulties to a large extent inherent in the concept itself. The first is change. In "Tradition
and the Individual Talent," Eliot says that each new work

modifies the total order in some small way; explaining that modification is Frye's most glaring weakness in his attempt to annotate Eliot's statement. The existing order in *Anatomy of Criticism* tends to be totalitarian, subsuming the work into its system of myths and archetypes. Frye can explain very well the mythic patterns shared by the *Odyssey* and *Ulysses;* he is less strong on how, and more importantly why, they differ on the use of those patterns. To say that *Ulysses* is different because it is a further displacement of the myths than its ancient counterpart is merely redundant. Yet, because Frye's universe is self-contained, he has no other means of explaining these differences; historical, political, philosophical, social—the whole spectrum of "extraliterary"—factors and exigencies are denied him as possible explanations. Similarly, Bloom, whose theory is one of change, can explain that change only in terms of the new poet's "anxiety of influence." Never does he suggest the possibility that the ephebe might reject the poetics of his precursors not only because he must establish his own voice, but also because he finds older poetics no longer adequate to deal with the world.

A second problem arises when the ostensibly heuristic categories become constitutive elements of "great literature" or "strong poetry." In speaking of "fictions like those of Trollope," Frye states:

> If . . . we go on to study the theme or total shape of the fictions, we find that it also belongs to a convention or category, like those of comedy or tragedy. With the literary category we reach a dead end, until we realize that literature is a reconstructed mythology, with its structural principles derived from those of myth. (FI, 38)

Now on the face of it, this statement seems innocent and descriptive enough, but if we look elsewhere, into the *Anatomy,* for instance, we find its prescriptive underside:

> This coincides with a feeling we have all had: that the study of mediocre works of art remains a random and peripheral form of critical experience, whereas the profound masterpiece

> draws us to a point at which we seem to see an enormous
> number of converging patterns of significance. (AC, 17)

No longer is it a simple matter of literature being a reconstructed mythology. Rather, we find a buried adjective, a
hidden value judgment: *good* literature is a reconstructed mythology, and the closer a work lies to its mythological patterns, the better it is. Mediocre works are mediocre not
through poor writing, weak plot, thin characters, shoddy
rhythms, but through their failure to play out certain accepted patterns of literary typology. Thus, it is entirely possible for a work to fulfill Frye's criterion for profound
masterpieces—that is, that it have "an enormous number of
converging patterns of significance"—and still be a work that
is quite without interest for its readers. Put another way, the
work might appear great at the considerable distance from it
that Frye urges the critic to adopt, at which only patterns can
be discerned, while looking worse and worse the closer the
reader approaches it. At the proximity of the actual reader, it
can be a catastrophe of bad writing and silliness, devoid of
any intelligible meaning. Frye simply assumes that his system can provide at once an accurate taxonomy and a means
for sorting out good from bad, without forcing the critic into
the (for him) distasteful practice of making value judgments
based on taste. His value judgments are based instead on an
objective, if not entirely measurable, criterion.

The chief beneficiary of his value judgment is the modern
work, the new, even the unwritten, for he points the way to
greatness for the aspiring creator of literature. Like Eliot, he
admits the new work into the ideal order of monuments at
once; there is no resistance, no tension, in Frye's theory between the old and the new. He even shows a distinct bias for
Modernist works. At the same time, however, those same
works become extremely problematic for him: they lead him
dangerously near tautology. Much of his theory of criticism
is based on an assumption that the critic can stand back farther from the work than the artist, who, involved as he is
with the moment-to-moment exigencies of creation, may not
be aware of the mythic patterns on which he draws, nor in-

deed must he be, so deeply ingrained are those patterns by his previous experience of literature. With the Modern work, such an assumption is clearly inaccurate; *The Waste Land* and *Ulysses*, for example, are keenly aware not only of the myths on which they draw but also of the ways in which those myths are displaced. In dealing with such self-consciously archetypal, mythic literature, Frye's archetypal, mythic criticism becomes precisely the sort of unpacking of the writer's literary valise that he is trying to avoid. Nor does saying that irony bottoms out into myth once again explain adequately what happens in these works, for the myth of *Ulysses* is not the same as the myth of the *Odyssey,* and the Tristan and Iseult of *Finnegans Wake* bear only limited resemblance to the original. "Quest and Cycle in *Finnegans Wake*," to pick a notable example of Frye's practical criticism, is valuable not as criticism so much as Baedeker, as map of surface phenomena, for in a work such as the *Wake* the mythic elements are the obvious, surface elements past which we must penetrate. Much the same thing can be said, as we shall see in the next chapter, of Frye on *The Waste Land*. Because the literary universe described in *Anatomy of Criticism* is so rigidly self-contained, there appears to be no suitable method of understanding the necessity of displacement or of "bottoming out" into myth except to say that it happens as part of a cycle larger than the works themselves. In order to move toward a more adequate explanation of the use of myths and other literature in Modern literature, we need to break down the battlements.

The criticism that most systematically assails the walls of poetic autonomy is, of course, Marxism. Fredric Jameson's attacks on Structuralism's closed system of language in *The Prison-House of Language* can be transferred almost directly to a closed literary system such as Frye's:

> The work would therefore be an equation whose variables we are free to fill in with whatever content or interpretive code we

chose. . . . Yet these alternatives, while indicating the virtuosity of the interpreter, point to some basic structural flaw, some almost allegorical slackness, in the concept of the method itself, for which the refusal of all privileged content amounts to a license to use any kind indifferently. (P-H, 195–196)[39]

. . . where [Russian Formalism] saw the coming into existence of the work as the latter's ultimate content, now the Structuralists read the content of a given work as Language itself, and this is no mere accident or idiosyncrasy on the part of the individual critic but rather a formal distortion inherent in the model itself. (P-H, 200–201)

These two passages point to prejudices inherent in Structuralism as well as in Frye's formalism, and in the objections to those prejudices, Jameson offers us a lever for working Marxist criticism against such formalism. The first is the refusal of any privileged content, the isolation of the work from the outside world. We have already seen how Frye cuts off literature from all that is not Literature in much the same way the Structuralists cut it off from all that is not Language. The second prejudice emanates from the first: if the work is cut off from everything except Language (or Literature) then the subject matter of the work must necessarily be Language (or Literature). Frye says as much in his essay on Stevens:

Stevens is of particular interest and value to the critical theorist because he sees so clearly that the only ideas the poet can deal with are those directly involved with, and implied by, his own writing: that, in short, "Poetry is the subject of the poem." (FI, p. 238)

Such a view of the poem's solipsism is evidence of the critic's (or the poet's, or both) reification of the work, of his cutting the poem off from its historical process and treating it as an autonomous object, in short, of his ideological bias.

As a counter to such reification and the superficial thinking it entails, Jameson offers Marxism as a genuinely critical, rather than ideological, system and as a heightening of thought:

> It is, of course, thought to the second power: an intensification
> of the normal thought process such that a renewal of light
> washes over the object of their [the critics'] exasperation, as
> though in the midst of its immediate perplexities the mind had
> attempted, by will power, by fiat, to lift itself mightily up by
> its own bootstraps. (M&F, 307)[40]

"Thought to the second power" means thinking about the historical and social origins of one's own thought as well as about the object of thought in and of itself. Thus the critic approaches the work through a critique of preexistent categories, resituates both the work itself and his own criticism within a determinant historical context. The critic can, by this objective approach, unmask the ideologies behind the literary work, that is, uncover the true nature of the event. Marxist criticism, then, is the attempt to apply this methodology, to look at literature dialectically in order to discover problems in its ideology and in the manifestations of that ideology, the work itself.

Marxist criticism as a science of ideologies is made possible because its nature is critical rather than ideological, because it is a genuine system of thought rather than a system of belief masquerading as a system of thought. Because it can account for its own presuppositions in a way ideological thought cannot, Marxism can undertake an examination of the hidden presuppositions of ideological thought. If, however, Marxism is itself ideological through and through, that is to say, if it is founded on a belief system whose historical origin it fails to recognize adequately—if it fails to be "thought to the second power"—then its claims as a purely critical mode of thought are seriously compromised. If we examine Marxist criticism as practiced by Jameson, Georg Lukács, and Raymond Williams in terms of that failure to account for its ideological basis, we then can proceed to an analysis of the effects of that failure on the way those critics view the literary work in general, and the Modernist work specifically, since Modernism itself stands as a challenge to that unrecognized origin and its concomitant assumptions.

Two statements by Jameson offer an introduction to the ideological nature of Marxism:

> What distinguishes such concepts [which see a renewal of our perception] philosophically from genuine dialectical thinking is of course their failure to account for the initial numbness of our perception in the first place, their inability to furnish a sufficiently historical explanation for that ontological deficiency which they can only understand in ethical and aesthetic terms. Yet such intellectual distortion, such structural repression of an essential element in the situation, is amply accounted for by the Marxist theory of ideology, which posits a kind of resistance of *mauvaise foi* that grows ever stronger as we draw closer and closer to that truth of the socio-economic which, were it realized in all its transparency, would immediately obligate us to praxis. (M&F, 374)

In this first passage, Jameson rests his case on a pair of tautologies to which he is blinded by his own masked ideology. The first tautology is that Marxism can offer historical explanation for the initial numbness of which Jameson speaks because, unlike other systems, it posits historical explanation as all encompassing. The implication that need not follow is that the Marxist conclusions are therefore superior, that the problem is remediable only if it is placed in its historical context, and not if it is *merely* identified and diagnosed. The second tautology follows from the first: if we can see the emptiness of an ideology we will be forced to adopt something else. Of course this is true, although it need not follow that the something else will be Marxism, any more than it necessarily follows that, as religious leaders are wont to tell us, the failure of one form of secular humanism or another must lead us back to the church. The masked ideology here is that Marxism is an ineluctable alternative to present ideologies, that it requires no act of conscious will but is automatic and inevitable:

> I believe it can be said that the only philosophically coherent alternative to such an interpretation out of the social substance

is one organized on a religious or theological basis, of which
Northrop Frye's system is only the most recent example. We
may therefore define religion as that set of imaginary propo-
sitions which must be believed if the theoretical consequences
of Marxism are to be avoided. (M&F, 402)

To suggest that *Anatomy of Criticism* or a kindred system is the
only alternative to Marxism is nonsense, but the analogy is
telling. Jameson's rhetoric here attempts to show the necessity of a "leap of faith" to religion in order to avoid the socialist consequences, which are logically unavoidable, just as
in the first passage he puts forth the notion of a perverse
resistance to truth by the intellect, so that it may elude similarly ineluctable consequences. Traditional Christian rhetoric
attempts to show the inevitability of God, the ineluctability
of belief, and like Jameson, that not to believe requires an act
of will, a leap of unfaith. What Jameson fails to recognize is
that, like Christianity, that set of principles to which he adheres is not a fact of existence but a belief system, that it does
require an active will-to-believe. This failure leads in turn to
a host of other problems.

One such problem is the failure of Marxism to see itself as
the product of a historical moment, the middle of the last
century in England. More specifically, while the critics may
acknowledge their roots in that time and place, they go about
using their system as though it were ahistorical. To claim a
methodology is outside history, universally applicable, for
use on all theories, events, and works of art, to determine
their historical and cultural significance, is patently absurd.
Marxism can no more escape its origins and built-in prejudices than can the ideologies it attacks. It is a product of the
same set of circumstances (although a different reaction to
them, certainly) that produced British Utilitarianism. Its basic
notions about the perfectability of man, the value of mass
education, social evolution, or progress toward a goal (the
notion of telos shares something of the substance although
little of the optimism of Mary Baker Eddy's "Every day in
every way, things get better and better") are all profoundly
nineteenth-century ideas.

The system, then, has certain built-in biases, and a failure to recognize them can result in difficulties similar to those of which Jameson accuses Wayne Booth:

> Mr. Booth has thus something in common with the object of his criticism: for James also attempted to arrive at the universal laws governing the proper composition of the novel in general, and showed as little awareness of the historically conditioned nature of form. The difference is that James in doing so reflected his moment in history, whereas Mr. Booth does not. (M&F, 358–359)

This argument can be turned back on a good deal of Marxist criticism, of which Lukács is a representative, which valorizes the sort of literature produced in the mid-nineteenth century. It displays a decided preference for realistic fiction and for utilitarian literature, while denigrating art for art's sake in favor of art for something else's sake, art that can be used as a lever against something in the world. In Lukács, for instance, art is asked to become a socialist lever or, failing that, at least not become a lever against socialism, "non-rejection of socialism is a sufficient basis for realism."[41]

Furthermore, Lukács accepts only realistic fiction as valid, this despite the fact that literary realism has not been the dominant mode in over half of a century:

> A realistic work of art, however rich in detail, is always opposed to naturalism. But an artistic method which reduces the dialectical—social-and-individual—totality of human existence must relapse, as we have seen, into naturalistic arbitrariness. It will then be incapable of depicting distortion in human nature or in the individual's relationship to his environment—incapable, that is, of seeing distortion as distortion. (RT, 75)

He goes on to say that this distortion is inevitable under capitalism, but that Modernism is ultimately incapable of handling it properly because of a lack of critical distance. Evidently, he requires critical detachment to exist on the page itself, between the level of the action and the level of the narrator. Indeed, he demonstrates this requirement in his comments on subjectivity:

> The uncritical approach of modernist writers—and of some modern philosophers—reveals itself in their conviction that this subjective experience constitutes reality as such. That is why this treatment of time can be used by the realistic writer to characterize certain figures in his novels, although in a modernist work it may be used to describe reality itself. Again and again Thomas Mann places characters with a time-experience of this subjectivist kind in relation to characters whose experience of time is normal and objective. (RT, 51)

Lukács does not explain how a character in a novel can have an objective and normal experience of time. It would seem that a character, if realistic, can only experience time subjectively, although he may step back from his experience to try to formulate a theory of objective time. But he will never be able to experience time objectively. That is a contradiction in terms. Even the novelist cannot, but must attempt to picture objective time, and objective reality, by stepping out of his experience.

Lukács' observations on objectivity are related directly to the system he employs, which is historically conditioned to be out of step with his age. The very notion of a telos, a goal toward which man is moving inexorably and that exists outside him, is a product of the thinking of the 1840s and 1850s, and is a response to the subjectivity of Romanticism. No, say the Victorians, man is moving toward universal improvement and benefit (the greatest good for the greatest number). No, say the Marxists, man is moving toward freedom from economic oppression. The difference lies in the source of the movement: for the former it is a mixture of God-sent goodness and plain old English common sense and generosity; for the latter, the discontent of the working man. However, that they both sense a telos is indisputable. In failing, then, to recognize the historicity of those ideas, Lukács disqualifies himself (as do others) from being able to deal effectively with Modernist literature, in which (as a response to these preceding movements) the sense of the future is much less clear.

A second problem arises from the ideological notion of telos when the Marxists attempt to deal with Modernism: the concept of imminent collapse. The manifest future envisioned in communist theory leads critics to see their age as perched on the brink of demise, as bourgeois civilization burns itself up with the new proletarian society rising out of its ashes. A prerequisite of this state of affairs, however, is a demonstration of the decline of society to its current precipice. The first step here is the positing of a past "golden age" in which external things were seen as a product of human activity and thought and action were unified:

> For Aristotle, the emotional satisfaction of tragedy is easily divided into its functional components of pity and fear, which attach to fate witnessed and thereby purge individual and community alike of their own social and existential anxiety. Such a final cause of tragedy is therefore able to serve a social function in its very nature. (M&F, 394–395)

In other words, Aristotle's audience went to the theater to be purged of social anxieties, to see a society that was worse off than its own, to be taken to the brink of disaster in the fall of the hero and then resolve its crises after the fall. The next step is to oppose modern abstraction against past concreteness: "In contrast, pleasure under capitalism is simply the sign of the consumption of an object: it is thus relatively extraneous to the objects' structure or use, since it can attach to any kind of object, and is at the same time gratuitous that it serves no collective function beyond that of encouraging further consumption and making the system operate at top capacity" (M&F, 395).

Jameson does not show how he arrives at the notion that the pleasure derived from watching a modern production is necessarily degraded. He simply states it, as he does the first half of the argument, assuming that his audience, sharing his beliefs, can fill in the required logic. His notion of the ancients' possessing a unified culture, in which individual and whole, religion and government, economics and art were inextricably tied, in which the playgoer would be so in tune

with his experience that dramatic Thebes became indistinguishable from real Thebes, thereby provoking genuine pity
and fear, rather than the degraded forms of pity and fear the
modern audience pretends at, is a pernicious form of the
"noble savage" argument, which equates ancient with prim-
itive and unsophisticated.

Raymond Williams indulges in a variation of teleological
distortion in his discussion of tragedy:

> The ages of comparatively stable belief, and of comparatively
> close correspondence between beliefs and actual experience,
> do not seem to produce tragedy of any intensity, though of
> course they enact the ordinary separations and tensions and
> the socially sanctioned ways of resolving these. The intensifi-
> cation of this common procedure, and the possibility of its
> permanent interest, seem to depend more on an extreme ten-
> sion between belief and experience than on an extreme cor-
> respondence. Important tragedy seems to occur neither in
> periods of real stability, nor in periods of open and decisive
> conflict. Its most common historical setting is the period pre-
> ceding the substantial breakdown and transformation of an
> important culture.[42]

This seemingly innocuous and neutral observation on the
historical nature of tragedy takes on added significance when
looked at in context, as the jumping-off point for a book on
modern tragedy. The false syllogism behind that statement
goes something like this: important tragedy precedes cultural
breakdowns; modern tragedy is important; modern culture is
about to break down. This is specious. Williams demonstrates neither causality nor necessity, and his error stems
from his ideology. His sense of telos requires that he see
bourgeois culture as ready to collapse, so he seeks to show
that it is producing significant tragedy (despite the claims of
other critics, who say it is not producing tragedy at all, but
pathos). Williams' problem here, as with the other problems
encountered in Marxist criticism, is that his ideology blinds
him to certain aspects of the thing criticized, so that while
some genuinely valuable observations are made, much is fal-
sified or ignored, so that we may ask with Lukács "not: is x

present in reality? But rather: does x represent the whole of reality? Again, the question is not: should x be excluded from literature? But rather: should we be content to leave it as x?" (RT, 45). The question becomes not Has something been accurately observed? but Has that which has not been observed affected that which has? Ideology is something critics bring to the work. When a system that claims to be a "science of ideologies," however, fails to account for its own ideological nature, a priori biases masquerade as objective analyses.

Williams' failure to account for the historical origin of his own thought distorts his analysis of *Women in Love* as a modern tragedy:

> The turning away from the social dimension is also, and inevitably, a turning away from persons. It is an attempt to create the individual person without any relationships. . . . when we arrive at that final division, between society and individual, we must know that an assertion of belief in either is irrelevant. What has actually happened is a loss of belief in both, and this is our way of saying a loss of belief in the whole experience of life, as men and women live it. This is certainly the deepest and most characteristic form of tragedy in our century. (MT, 183)

Here Williams is doing what a number of commentators before him have done, focusing on a single character at a single point in the novel as Lawrence's spokesman, Birkin, on the "two stars at polar opposition." Williams is doing so to grind his ideological axe: his sense of imminent collapse of the existing society urges him to focus on only one aspect of the novel. This is a profoundly undialectic way to read Lawrence, particularly in light of the complex system of dualism, in which no element is defined by itself, in isolation, but always in opposition to another element. Relationships between things, and between people, are immensely important in Lawrence, and he would agree that the individual without any relationships is the deepest form of tragedy, in this or any other century. That is not, however, the plight of the living at the end of *Women in Love*, as Williams maintains. Rather, life without relationships is the downfall of Gerald, who becomes more and more enamored of the cold isolation of the Tyrol until it kills him. Birkin and Ursula return to the world of relationships, to England, and at the end are discussing not how to live in proud singleness, but what kinds of relationships are needed for a fulfilling life.

Lukács also suffers from this affliction, although his is frequently related to nostalgia rather than telos:

> And though Kafka's artistic method differs from that of other modernist writers, the principle of presentation is the same: the world is an allegory of transcendant Nothingness. . . . To sum up our inquiry so far: similarity of technique does not imply similarity of ideology; nor is the approval or rejection of certain techniques a pointer to a writer's basic aim. (RT, 53)

Lukács castigates Kafka for not being Hoffmann, for not using his realism to depict an ideology not of his own time. In finding the replacement of telos with Nothingness unacceptable, Lukács conforms with Marxist ideology, but he flies in its face by saying form does not bear a necessary relationship to content. In this, he has reverted to the pre-Marxist conception of form and matter, in which the latter is inert, rather than the mutually active form and content Jameson discusses. Lukács here adheres strictly to one part of his ideology, so much so that it conflicts with another part.

Furthermore, he, like Williams, is eager to see man portrayed in modernist literature without relationships, cut off not only from other human contact but from history as well:

> First, the hero is strictly confined within the limits of his own experience. There is not for him—and apparently not for his creator—any preexistent reality beyond his own self, acting upon him or being acted upon by him. Secondly, the hero himself is without personal history. He is "thrown into the world": meaninglessly, unfathomably. He does not develop through contact with the world; he neither forms nor is formed by it. The only "development" in this literature is the gradual revelation of the human condition. (RT, 21)

Again, the hero in total isolation is the great characteristic of Modernism for the Marxists, who wish to see in the collapse of relationships the symptoms of the breakdown of modern society. So Lukács sees isolation everywhere in modern literature. We have already seen that Lawrence does not subscribe to the solipsism; and turning to that other pillar of modern British fiction, Joyce, we find that neither does he. In *Ulysses,* for example, characters are always and everywhere acted upon by other characters, by society, by personal and public history. Stephen is followed by the memory of his mother, Bloom by the ghosts of his father and son, Molly by her lovers, past and present. Nor are relationships confined to those with the dead. Stephen's poor relationship with his family drives him into the world, while the lack of human relationships has brought him back to Dublin. Molly's affair with Boylan does affect Bloom, while his scheming in turn affects both her and Stephen. Characters interact on a psychosocial level to produce, as collective expressions, the lofty rhetoric of the Cyclops episode and the fugue of the Sirens. For every human action in *Ulysses,* there is a corresponding reaction; characters do not exist in isolation but always in relation to other characters.

Finally, a serious methodological problem is posed by Marxist ideology. Critics can take only an extrinsic approach to literature: how does a piece of literature fit into its historical setting? what problems does it point out in society? what answers does it pose to the problems? In short, Marxism wants to study literature as if it were philosophy or sociology and to deny its artistic elements. Only the most general formal considerations are admitted, and then merely as they apply to the philosophy of the work. Lukács' comments on symbolism and allegory point up this weakness: "Allegory is that aesthetic genre which lends itself par excellence to a description of man's alienation from objective reality. Allegory is a problematic genre because it rejects that assumption of immanent meaning to human existence which . . . is the basis of traditional art" (RT, 40).

In pressing for a one-to-one obvious correspondence between the work of art and the world outside, he fails to see that allegory, and symbolism (which he seemingly includes as a subspecies) are not a turning away from the outer world but another method of illustrating the relationship. Moreover, the structural unity that can accrue from symbolic use can strengthen not only the work but its philosophical content as well. Symbolism is not "an infallible sign that his thinking—or the thinking of the class which he represents, in the sense of its social development—does not dare penetrate the reality which lies before its eyes" (M&F, 337) but may indeed be a more potent way of penetrating that reality.

It turns out, then, that the weaknesses of Marxist criticism are most glaring in light of Modernist literature, which is a reaction against the age of which Marxism is a product. In failing to recognize the historically conditioned basis of its method, as well as that of the movement under critique, Marxism factors an equation with one element missing, and until all the elements are considered, the results of that equation will be skewed.

It should be clear by this point that, despite their differences, the preceding theories (and all others, including *this* one) share a tendency to observe literature with blinders on, to engage it on preselected levels. In recent years, another school of critical thought has arisen to attempt to deal with the matter of blind spots, textual and critical entanglements, misreadings, and what constitutes a reading or a misreading. That movement, of course, is Deconstruction. With the possible exception of Structuralism, no movement since the New Criticism has generated so much debate, discussion, and outright rancor.

Like Structuralism, Deconstruction holds attraction for literary critics in its highly specialized, pseudoscientific vocabulary. Always nervous about the apparent lack of standards by which other disciplines can be judged, the literary community, or at least part of it, has been quick to latch onto any theory that offers the possibility of systematic, rather than individual, rigor. Unlike Structuralism, the school of Derrida and followers has turned away from developing overarching explanations of how literature fits together, concentrating instead on those elements that do not fit, that threaten the unity, the coherence, that Structuralism, like other formalisms, seeks to find. As Jonathan Culler puts it, "deconstruction arrives in the wake of structuralism to frustrate its systematic projects."[43] In medical terms, Structuralism is anatomy, Deconstruction pathology. The former studies how things fit together and what makes them go; the latter, what makes them go wrong.

Most deconstructionists and commentators on the movement are in agreement as to its closely analytical nature, which is perhaps most succinctly and clearly stated by Barbara Johnson:

> *Deconstruction* is not synonymous with *destruction*, however. It is in fact much closer to the original meaning of the word *analysis*, which etymologically means "to undo"—a virtual synonym for "to de-construct." The de-construction of a text does not proceed by random doubt or arbitrary subversion, but by the careful teasing out of warring forces of signification within the text itself. If anything is destroyed in a deconstructive reading, it is not the text, but the claim to unequivocal domination of one mode of signifying over another. A deconstructive reading is a reading that analyzes the specificity of a text's critical difference from itself.[44]

The difference of which she speaks alludes to Derrida's concept *différance* (a coinage of his), which he explains as simultaneously passive and active, a being and a doing that "is the systematic play of differences, of traces of differences, of the spacing by which elements relate to one another."[45]

The emphasis on differences, on "warring forces" within texts, immediately separates deconstruction from other formalisms. Where the New Critics seek to demonstrate the organic unity of literary works, their wholeness or oneness with themselves; where Frye, after Eliot, outlines the oneness not of individual works but of the entire canon, the whole graveyard full of monuments; where the Structuralists elaborate the unity of works as the play of more or less homogeneous signifiers and fundamental, repeated oppositions—here, the Deconstructionists set out to show that the text (literary, critical, philosophical, psychological, nearly any text may suit) pushes ceaselessly against the limits of that alleged unity. The basic operation of Deconstruction is to dismantle the text, the discourse, examining the ways it undercuts its premises, how its rhetoric battles against its structure or announced program (*OD*, 86).

Beyond this basic set of assumptions, however, there is relatively little consensus regarding who is a Deconstructionist or what exactly the proper activity for such a critic may be. Both the movement itself and its detractors have pegged Harold Bloom as a Deconstructive critic, a label he seemed to authorize when, several years ago, he edited a collection of writings by several of the Yale luminaries entitled, suggestively enough, *Deconstruction*. Lately, however, he has been at great pains to suggest that not only is he not a Deconstructionist, but that no critic raised and schooled in America really could be.[46] Numerous other critics have seemed to agree, suggesting that whatever the mass of American critics are doing in their analyses of literary texts, it is not *really* Deconstruction.[47]

Bloom, for his part, goes even further in insisting on his separation when, in *The Breaking of the Vessels*, he asserts the existence of a gulf between the activities of the literary critic and thinkers of the Derridean school:

> That something other may be very valuable; it may be philosophy or scholarship or a human science, but it will not be personal, agonistic, and original. Perhaps that something other, whether as theory or as praxis, will be more socially useful than literary criticism, more involved in the relations of history and society, and in the realms of discourse not aesthetic. So be it. But if its language be that of Hegel and Heidegger, of Derrida and Foucault, it will be a language of being and knowledge, or the absence of being and knowledge. Is *this* [Bloom's text] the language of being and knowledge, present or absent, or the language of the will, of action and desire, possession and power. Is this criticism, and if not, what are you preferring to it?[48]

There is justice in his claims here, despite the self-aggrandizement. What literary critics, particularly those of the Anglo-American tradition, find off-putting in the work of Derrida and company is precisely that insistence that their method works equally well on fiction and philosophy, poetry and propaganda. Substantive differences do exist between those modes of discourse, and the New Critics never attempted to demonstrate the organic unity of, say, *Beyond Good and Evil* or the play of ambiguity/tension/paradox of Kant's *Analytic of the Beautiful*. The danger exists, moreover, that *Women in Love* or "Kubla Khan" in the hands of a Deconstructionist, or at least a clumsy one, will become no more than a tract available for debunking. On the other hand, those works have withstood a good deal of handling by all manner of critics, clumsy and otherwise.

The more serious charge Bloom levels here, however, deserves fuller answer. If Deconstruction is not literary criticism (whatever that may be), then what good is it? One may ask the same question of Structuralism, Marxism, even of Bloom's own Freudianism. Indeed, the now-discredited New Criticism is the only modern body of critical writing that develops from a *literary* background or whose principal exponents have been creators of primary works of poetry and fiction with an interest in demonstrating how literature is put together from the ground up. If one of the sins of the New Critics has been to place too great a value on literary creation, these other theories have moved in just the opposite direction. In each case, they attempt to show the poet or novelist not as hero but as victim: of ideology, of inherent structures, of literary tradition, of psychological forces larger than himself. Like these others, Deconstruction underprivileges the creative act by showing the ways in which writers are unable to marshall all their linguistic forces along the same lines.

Much as its practitioners and theorists claim neutrality, Deconstruction reveals in its own rhetoric an antithetical relationship to whatever text it may engage. The emphasis on texts "undermining" their own philosophy or hierarchical operations (*OD*, 86) or containing "warring factions" that critics can tease out immediately puts the critic in an adversarial relation to the text at hand. Perhaps for that reason, much recent deconstructive criticism has focused on texts that deliberately play on ambiguity, or that deconstruct themselves. Indeed, the subtitle of Ralph Flores' *Rhetoric of Doubtful Authority* is *Deconstructive Readings of Self-Questioning Narratives, St. Augustine to Faulkner.* It may be that Deconstructive analyses are most fruitful when performed on texts that tend to deconstruct themselves. Until we have seen more of this new movement, until it has undergone a period of shakedown, we cannot be sure.

Perhaps more to the point, and here Flores' study is exemplary, Deconstruction seems best suited to engaging not literary texts themselves but other critics on those texts. In his chapter on *Absalom, Absalom!,* Flores examines the role of the half-breed, particularly in the figure of Charles Bon, in subverting the binary opposition of black and white. Bon is never really seen but instead is conjured by the various narrators and is a reflection (often indeed shown as a reflection) of their obsessions and biases. His presence then becomes problematic, necessarily forcing misreading, misinterpretation by those narrators, leading them into the narratives as players, catching them in the web they seek to stand above and analyze. The implications for the reader of Faulkner's novel are clear: we can no more avoid the entanglement than can Miss Rosa or Quentin, and our reading, like theirs, must be a misreading. Flores further argues, rather persuasively, that any totalizing critical narrative (he cites John Irwin's *Doubling and Incest/Revenge and Repetition* largely because of its emphasis on binary opposition) must be doomed to failure by the complexity of the novel, by the disunity brought about through the narrative self-questioning.

Similarly, in a long and exquisitely argued essay, "Turning the Screw of Interpretation," Shoshana Felman deconstructs not merely James's novella but the critical debate that has raged for decades. Taking Edmund Wilson's at-one-time-startling assertion that the governess is mad as a starting point, she examines both that position and its opposite, that the ghosts are real. Neither account of the story, however, deals adequately with James's assertions, both in letters and the New York edition Preface, as well as ample evidence in the text itself, that the tale is ambiguous, nonresolving. Instead of accepting either argument, Felman puts forth one of her own, that the reader is trapped into one stance or the other by the story's narrative strategy, that "*The Turn of the Screw* imposes the governess's distorted point of view upon us as the rhetorical *condition* of our perception of the story. In James's tale as in Hoffmann's [*The Sandman*], madness is uncanny, *unheimlich*, to the precise extent that it cannot be situated, coinciding, as it does, with the very space of reading." [49] That is, the reader cannot be outside the text, or at least cannot be sure of it: to choose is to be controlled by the text (although perhaps not to choose is, too).

Ultimately, then, Deconstruction involves a return to close analysis of the text, although perhaps with a difference. Quite apart from New Critical close reading, for instance, where the particulars added up to an organic whole, Deconstructive emphasis on ambiguity or tension attempts to demonstrate the flaws in the larger design. Culler speaks of this tendency, "Instead of using literary works to develop a poetics of narrative, for example, the critic will study individual novels to see how they resist or subvert the logic of narrative" (*OD*, 220). The emphasis on subverting narrative (or poetic, or discursive) logic extends to the individual work's internal logic as well as to the logic of, say, Romantic poetics.

Such a critical revisionism seems a necessary and commonsensical element of the critical process, as a salutary companion to the general foolishness in which we all find ourselves caught periodically, if not ceaselessly. Moreover, such a mode of analysis precludes no other political or philosophical stance, so that one may be a Marxist or feminist or (presumably) reactionary Deconstructionist. Moreover, stripped of its Derridean jargon, Deconstructive criticism looks surprisingly familiar. The differences, for instance, between Felman's discussion of James and my own analysis of *The Waste Land* and its critical reception in the following chapter may be a matter more of style than substance, despite the fact that I make no claim to being a Deconstructionist.

Nevertheless, there is something limited and limiting about the program the Deconstructionists set for themselves. For one thing, it almost necessarily relies on other readings against which to work its magic. In Culler's example of narrative poetics, for instance, deconstruction requires the prior concept of a poetics of prose in order to show how a given work may subvert that logic, just as Felman requires Wilson or Flores requires Irwin. Fair enough, there is no paucity of competing readings of any text; still, the stance and rhetoric of this secondary or even tertiary analysis suggests its privileged nature, despite the insistence that readings are not privileged over texts, that readers inevitably must be implicated in the act of reading, that they become coconspirators with the authors.

Behind this cavil, moreover, lies a more substantive concern: Deconstruction has no means of generating systematic understanding of literary works or movements. A novel or a poem, like any writing, is an imperfect creation of an imperfect creator. That warring forces will be at work within it should hardly come to us as news. A system designed for showing us those differences within serves a valuable and useful purpose. Can it also show us the similarities between? Can it tell us, for instance, whether "Kubla Khan" is more like "Tintern Abbey" or *Women in Love?* Can it demonstrate affinities despite the differences? The evidence to date suggests otherwise. Perhaps this failing is no failing; perhaps, I am asking that an apple be a melon. Or, perhaps, there are possibilities in Deconstruction not yet tapped. We must conclude, however, that despite the value of Deconstructive criticism in revising our readings, in changing notions of given works, it is not an all-encompassing system. It can operate only, it seems, as part of a multiplicity of critical activities, as a critical watchdog, a debunker of grand schemes. Perhaps, that is plenty.

This discussion of critical theories has proceeded along the lines of several implicit principles, and it is essential that, before looking at the Modernist works themselves, these principles be given voice and set in motion as an active force. They will not cohere into a uniform system so much as a foundation on which to build. In fact, one of the conclusions they lead to is that theory, at the point at which it becomes system, subsumes its subject into itself and becomes the center of its own interest, something I wish to avoid in this study.

1. The literary work does not exist independent of its contexts: social, historical, or literary.

2. At the same time, neither does it assume a subservient role to those contexts.

These first two points enable any further literary examination; they are at once inseparable and worthy of separate consideration. What the preceding theoretical analyses have attempted to demonstrate is that in one way or another the major critical theories of this century have reinforced the split between the literary work and its context, particularly its social context. Even Marxism, which argues against the form and content split it finds in bourgeois criticism and which extends the notion of form and content outside the work to the work in society, actually lends further support to the separation. By privileging society over the work, literature becomes less an element of society that somehow works within society than a symptom of society's health or sickness. Marxism shares with the systems it critiques a tacit assumption that the work of art, particularly the work of art under capitalism, is a product, a commodity, an object. The sociological approach forces those who would resist it into theories of artistic autonomy; nineteenth-century literary criticism is a case in point. So long as the work is seen as an object, it will require that we understand it either as a product of its society, as a sociological artifact, or else cut off entirely from that society. This dilemma leads us to the third consideration.

3. *Work* is also a verb. Thus, the literary work is better understood as a process of carving out a space for itself

within the various historical situations it confronts than as an object or a product. Conceiving it as a process obviates the possibility of a form–content split. That split occurs because we see two objects, a text contained on a page, or in a book (that text is an object, an entity held between covers), and a society that appears quite independent of, or oblivious to, the text. The text therefore must be a product of the larger, intractable object, or it must assume a similarly oblivious attitude, if it is to retain its autonomy as a thing in itself. In viewing the literary work as a process, however, we move toward a vision of the text not only as an object before our eyes but also as pretext, or text in the act of becoming. That is to say, the work is not only that apparently finished product lying before us but also the encounter of the individual writer with his social, personal, and literary histories and with the problems or situations he is attempting to work out through his writing. The writing itself becomes an attempt to somehow mediate between self and world.

4. Literary creation, then, is not a wholly private act either in its origins or its goals. It is not written in a vacuum, however attractive the lonely artist in his tower has become as an image of the modern artist, since even this cloistering of the artist is a social act (or rather, perhaps, an antisocial act). Moreover, a book or poem will not be aimed at every potential reader, yet its attempt to reach one audience—and exclude another—is also a social act. Joyce may have hoped his book would keep the scholars busy for decades, but he did not hope it would be unread. The writer shapes his writing with his goals in mind, and while he may select elements that shock or dismay or perplex his readers, it seems extremely unlikely that he makes his selection based on those elements' inferior ability to achieve his goals.

5. Form, therefore, is not merely an internal device acting within the work. Rather, it is an element of the process; it is "the poem of the mind in the act of finding what

will suffice." The Victorian novel, with its socially and economically ordained form, and the Modern novel, with its constant searching after suitable form, are nevertheless similar in that their uses of form are part of the process of carving out their relationships to their societies and to their own literary antecedents. Only when the reader reifies the works and internalizes his understanding of form do they become formally dissimilar. Form, finally, is as much an element of meaning as content, is equally a part of the social and historical interaction of the work, and is inseparable from content. Form without content is an abstraction; even the outline of a work, which is perhaps the most formally abstract writing possible, is not simply a shape without content. At the same time, content without form is also impossible; content cannot be presented without form. The process of writing is simultaneously an act of finding one's meaning and giving it shape.

My final two points are at once conclusions drawn from the first five and directions the critical studies of the individual Modernist works will attempt to follow.

6. I would argue these principles are necessary if a theory is to avoid, at the extremes, solipsism or sociology. Even granting their necessity, however, many methods are possible and indeed desirable within the work of a single critic: the relationship between society, literature, and the artist at work will suggest different approaches for different works, genres, periods, writers, even within the canon of a single writer. The critic's activity also is one of finding what will suffice. The critic who, like Brooks, grasps a single method as Truth and applies it promiscuously to every piece of literature he encounters, without examining the differences in context between one work and another, falsifies the nature of the experience of reading as well as of the creative process. This falsification is no less true of Bloom: can the only reason that one writer differs from his literary ancestor

(as if he had but one) possibly be the anxiety of influence? While the desire not to show influence too directly may well exert power over the writer's creativity, surely an equally compelling reason he "swerves" from his progenitor's methods is that those methods and that style no longer are adequate to the world as he understands it. These are specific examples of the falsification that inevitably results from the translation of critical principles into overarching system. For system will ossify, bending its subject of study to accommodate itself rather than remaining pliant to the special needs of its subject. System tends to become object, to reify itself, to become forgetful of its own origins while retaining the final product. As product, it has an interest in proving itself valid, and that interest leads to the ossification, the intractability of system to circumstance. Criticism, on the other hand, must remain process, must, in each new encounter with literature, rediscover its methods.

7. In order to avoid this ossification of system, the critical activity must begin with a fairly close attention to the text, to the work itself, for it is there that the nuances of the creative dialectics play themselves out. Attention to the work is a way of following critical principles without moving toward the sclerotic systematization of methodology that attends a too profound involvement with principles in isolation. So long as the critic allows the work to suggest a method of proceeding with his criticism of it, rather than allowing methodology to dictate an approach, he avoids the risk of falsifying the work to fit the system. The place to start, then, with our understanding of the creative dialectic is with the evidence that remains to us, with the text, and to understand that text as process, as the act of finding what will suffice.

2 / *The Waste Land* and the Great War

In a way not available to many literary works, T. S. Eliot's *The Waste Land* has controlled its own criticism. To be sure, nearly any work will exert influence over its critics' methods, but few have been able to dictate those methods with anything like the success of Eliot's great poem. While this is not to suggest that all critics are reduced to a single approach in dealing with the work, it is meant to imply that there are very strong trends in that body of criticism which the poem has spawned, and this is so for three reasons: the nature of the poem, the notes, and Eliot's work as a critic. The first two we shall encounter as we move into the poem, but any thorough understanding of the poem's relationship to its critics must begin with an understanding of Eliot's relationship as critic to those who follow him.

In several senses Eliot is the father of modern Formalist criticism. His statements in "Tradition and the Individual Talent" argue for a view of poetry as an autonomous world, a view subsequently adopted by a good deal of modern criticism:

> No poet, no artist of any art, has his complete meaning alone. His significance, his appreciation is the appreciation of his relation to the dead poets and artists. You cannot value him

alone; you must set him, for contrast and comparison, among the dead. I mean this as a principle of aesthetic, not merely historical, criticism. The necessity that he shall conform, that he shall cohere, is not one-sided; what happens when a new work is created is something that happens simultaneously to all the works of art which preceded it. The existing monuments form an ideal order among themselves, which is modified by the introduction of the new (the really new) work of art among them. The existing order is complete before the new work arrives; for order to persist after the supervention of novelty, the whole order must be, if ever so slightly, altered; and so the relations, proportions, values of each work of art toward the whole are readjusted; and this is conformity between the old and the new.[1]

Eliot removes art from its social context in this passage by killing it; by placing the living poet among the dead and his work in an "ideal order" of monuments, he removes from both poet and poetry the responsibility of corresponding to life. In saying that each new work of literature informs the existing order and is in turn informed by that order, he posits a self-contained literary universe in which the main concern is, ultimately, itself. That he succeeds is indicated by the continuing flow of criticism that states, with Eugenia M. Gunnar in *T. S. Eliot's Romantic Dilemma, "The Waste Land,* published in final form three years after the publication of 'Tradition and the Individual Talent,' may be treated as the poetic equivalent of the ideas presented in that critical work" (104). Of course, he is not the first to view literature in such a manner; in the century preceding the publication of "Tradition and the Individual Talent," Arnold's touchstone theory and Pater's art for art's sake, as well as the work of the Symbolists, outlined similar theories. And like Pater and the Symbolists, Eliot is motivated in his theory, in part at least, by a reaction against the nineteenth-century political-aesthetic philosophy that saw literature as a social weapon and that still existed in 1919 in the work of the New Humanists, among others. Whereas Arnold, however, proposes an idea more than a system of thought, and whereas Pater and the Symbolists are more concerned with a program for poets than a critical system, Eliot puts forth the basis for a coherent critical method in his essay, a new line of aesthetic criticism. Further, his extensive body of practical criticism, which has been so effective in changing critical evaluations of poets and periods in the last half-century, adds considerable force to his theory.

That his theory meets with success is attested to by the fact that eleven years later Edmund Wilson must deal with Eliot the critic in his discussion of Eliot the poet:

> Eliot and Valery follow Coleridge and Poe in their theory as well as in their verse, and they seem to me to confuse certain questions by talking as if the whole of literature existed simultaneously in a vacuum, as if Homer's and Shakespeare's situations had been the same as Mallarme's and Laforgue's, as if the latter had been attempting to play the same sort of roles as the former and could be judged on the same basis.[2]

What Wilson attacks is precisely that sense of tradition Eliot pushes for, the simultaneous existence of monuments. Of course, as a modern poet, Eliot has a vested interest in such thinking; the admission of Mallarme and Laforgue—and, by extension, Joyce and Eliot—into literary journals and university curricula alongside Homer and Shakespeare greatly enhances the respectability of the modern artist. It removes from consideration questions of popularity and places the artist instead in the protected, comparatively changeless world of the academy. It is not really the monumentalization of his work that is at issue. One recalls Shakespeare confidently proclaiming that his sonnet will outlast the great statues. Eliot, however, is perhaps the first to need so badly to accomplish it during his own lifetime. While Shakespeare's claim acts as a proof against the oblivion of death and the amnesia of the future, Eliot's acts as a proof against the ignominy of the present. In nearly every major statement of his career—his famous retrenchments in politics and religion; his nostalgia for a time before the dissociation of sensibility; his desire to have his own work set beside that of the old masters—Eliot shows himself reacting against the flow of the modern world, and his theory of tradition allows his work to

be placed within the tradition not only by the activity of subsequent critics, but also by the sort of poetry such a theory
leads him to create. The notion of tradition works itself out
in his poetry as a style heavily laden with allusions, parodies,
and quotations, and by the notes to *The Waste Land*.

To a greater degree, perhaps, than his critical writings,
Eliot determines the direction of modern criticism by adding
the notes to *The Waste Land*. His initial impulse to include
notes seems to stem from his notion of a poetic continuum or
ideal order, that the new poem draws on and adds to earlier
poems, and that, by extension, the poem will not be understood completely if its specific antecedents are not recog-
nized. The notes also manifest a concern to demonstrate that
the poem is a product of erudition, design, and control,
rather than of madness and chaos, a concern which takes on
special significance in the face of the decay and collapse of
modern society discussed in the poem. Indeed, *The Waste
Land* can be read as an attempt to protect the poet from the
decadence it depicts (although, I believe, that part of the attempt fails), as if the poem, by identifying the problems of
relativism, fragmented consciousness, and spiritual dryness,
can shelter him from their effects. Ultimately, Eliot finds himself implicated by his own methods, but the desire for protec-
tion remains nevertheless, and it expresses itself in the notes,
which continue the monumentalizing (along different lines,
however) that fails in the poem. The importance of the notes,
however, rests at least as much with the critics as with the
poet, and in this connection the most crucial is the unnum-
bered headnote:

> Not only the title, but the plan and a good deal of the inciden-
> tal symbolism of the poem were suggested by Miss Jessie L.
> Weston's book on the Grail legend: *From Ritual to Romance*
> (Cambridge). Indeed, so deeply am I indebted, Miss Weston's
> book will elucidate the difficulties of the poem much better
> than my notes do; and I recommend it (apart from the great
> interest of the book itself) to any who think such elucidation
> worth the trouble. To another work of anthropology I am in-

debted in general, one which has influenced our generation profoundly; I mean *The Golden Bough;* I have used especially the two volumes *Adonis, Attis, Osiris.* Anyone who is acquainted with these works will immediately recognize in the poem certain references to vegetative ceremonies.[3]

This note, along with those that follow it, has controlled criticism of the poem, and of modern literature in general, for over fifty years. Nor is this merely incidental; Eliot offers, at a propitious moment in literary history, a method that allows criticism an opportunity to create monuments of its own. That criticism had need of such an act is largely a function of the rise of the sciences: over the last half century or so, critics have expressed the desire to put their endeavors on a par with the sciences, to "make criticism scientific," by which they generally mean, in Northrop Frye's words, "rigorous and systematic." Humanistic disciplines, in an increasingly scientific and technological society, find themselves the poor cousins. Eliot's notes extend to criticism the possibility of a systematic, nonimpressionistic method analogous to the methods of the sciences, a method that finds its eventual apotheosis forty years later in *Anatomy of Criticism.*

More than any other single critic, Frye is indebted to Eliot's notion of tradition as a simultaneous structure, and he is at pains to acknowledge the debt in the *Anatomy.* Not surprisingly, then, when he turns his attention to *The Waste Land,* which more than any other of Eliot's poems incorporates that same notion into its design, he follows very closely the mode of analysis that the poem implicitly, and the notes explicitly, suggest. The method Frye adopts in dealing with the poem involves first of all distancing himself from the content, from the "raw material" of the poem as much as possible. This distancing he accomplishes by focusing his discussion on consciously literary aspects: the Grail legend, the citations, the patterns of imagery. To explain the passage in which the crowds stream across London Bridge, for example, Frye notes that Eliot "repeats another line from the same Canto 3: 'I had not thought death had undone so many.' Most of the people are coming out of tube-stations, and the subway is a good image for this waste-land world because, like Dante's scene, it is just below the surface of the ground."[4] The tenor of this statement, like most of Frye's comments on the poem, suggests that the poem is of interest because of the way it fits itself into the larger category of the existing monuments— here, how the subway is a good version of Dante's Hell— rather than how or why the poem incorporates those borrowings into itself and turns them to its own ends.

Moreover, Frye's reliance on a method that rests so heavily on sources outside the poem leads him to conclusions that are not entirely supported by the poem itself: "the Thames carries the filth of London into the sea, where we meet Phlebas again, and the healing waters return as rain at the end, reminding us of the symbolism of baptism in Christianity"(62). Both the river's cleansing of the city and the healing waters' return are debatable, since the poem shows us neither the cleansed city (only the polluted river) nor the rains themselves (only their promise). As Anne Wright notes in *Literature of Crisis, 1910–1922,* "Destruction and regeneration, death and rebirth, are held in tension by a strongly marked movement *towards* rebirth and regeneration (or however the 'solution' is characterised) but not *beyond* death and destruction" (187). By reading the poem through the filter of Literature, as it were, Frye transforms the poem into a sort of clearinghouse for death-and-rejuvenation myths. He is not, of course, without justification. Those myths are all there; Eliot acknowledges them in the notes, puts them in the poem. But what happens, it seems, in an Eliot-conditioned reading of the poem is that rather than reading those elements of the work through the work itself, the work is redistributed among its elements. The defect in Frye's approach, the approach the poet himself validates, is not so much the method as the order of priorities. There really is no question that those citations, allusions, and parodies are in the poem. But what are they doing there? How do they advance or subvert the poet's impulses, and how are they made appropriate to the business of the poem?

If we are to answer these questions about the poem, then

we must adopt a more dynamic view of the creative act than the commodity structure Frye's system[5] allows: reading the poem becomes a de-construction in the root sense offered by Barbara Johnson, an attempt to recapture the dialectic encounter of the poet with society and history, with those forces larger than himself of which he must try to make sense.

Alternately cause célèbre, opportunity, calamity, symbol, or indictment of the system, World War I served as a source of material for virtually every American writer of the late teens and early twenties. Its influence extended from popular songs to novels by practically every important writer of the time to the poetry of Pound's *Hugh Selwyn Mauberley* and, of course, *The Waste Land*. Eliot's poem, however, represents a different aspect of the war: not the war as experience, not the war as ideology, not the war as capitalistic tool, but the war as effect. The reader sees neither an immediate image of the war itself nor the underlying philosophies and prewar power struggles. Rather, he sees the effects of the war on English and European culture. Eliot makes it nearly impossible, moreover, to identify the war as the lone source of any single passage, by two elements of his poetic method. For one thing, he rarely alludes directly to the war. Second, his presentation is not one of cause and effect but of effect only; that is, he gives the reader a portrait of the condition or situation as it exists, with little or no authorial explication regarding the forming of the situation. Indeed, one may well say, with Harriet Davidson's *T. S. Eliot and Hermeneutics*, the poem lacks *any* coherent center and therefore lends itself not to meaning but to interpretation.[6] At the same time, this presentation of an ambiguous present, due to its very nature, cannot close off the possibility that the war is a major source of the conditions presented in the poem. Much of the imagery of the poem can be tied to the effects of the war on the fabric of European society. While these ties are suggestive rather than concrete, an examination of the poem in terms of them might lead to a different way of understanding not only the poem's relation to recent history but to its literary history as well.

Paul Fussell has suggested the connection between the poem and the war in *The Great War and Modern Memory*, indicating it was

> more profoundly a "memory of the war" than one had thought. Consider its archduke, its rats and canals and dead men, its focus on fear, its dusty trees, its conversation about demobilization, its spiritualist practitioners reminding us of those who preyed on relatives anxious to contact their dead boys, and not least its settings of blasted landscape and ruins, suggestive of what Guy Chapman recalls as "the confluent acne of the wasteland under the walls of Ypres."[7]

Fussell's comments offer a starting point for a discussion of the relation between the war and the poem, although they do not (nor do they presume to) deal with the poem in its entirety. The elements he notes are surface developments (he is more interested, after all, in the poem as literary sociology than as an individual work of art), whereas the poem is so often concerned with breaking through surfaces, with mythological correlatives to current conditions. To locate the war firmly in the poem requires the reader to marry Fussell's provocative suggestion to the archetypal criticism the poem seems to demand.

Perhaps one of the most important effects of the war on *The Waste Land* is its effect on the poet himself. The war did not have the same impact on Eliot that it had on so many young American and British artists, because he did not fight. He did volunteer but was turned down by the Navy and the Intelligence Service on medical grounds.[8] Therefore, his perception of the conflict is not one of first-hand experience on the battlefield, but rather one of witnessing the results of that conflict at home in England. Like Pound, and for that matter nearly everyone living in Europe during the war, Eliot had friends and acquaintances killed in battle. While the loss of these friends fails to show up directly in his writings, as it does in Pound's or Yeats's, Eliot was still distressingly aware of the young, promising, creative men who went off to war and did not return. Indeed, one suspects the often hysterical tone of his postwar poems to be rooted in the suppression of his knowledge of the war and its effects and in his refusal to deal with it directly. The loss of that creativity and fertility, as well as the accompanying spiritual dryness, manifests itself in a number of ways in the poem, from the title itself to the final image of the ruined tower and the benediction of peace, and in fact it continues to manifest itself in "The Hollow Men."

The first striking manifestation of war and death imagery, of course, is in the superstructure of the poem, in the title and the section headings. The title itself sets the tone of the work, and the central theme becomes that of the wasteland: dry, rocky, barren, with its attendant cultural stagnation and barrenness. If barrenness and destruction are set forth in the title, they become even more explicit in the five section headings: "The Burial of the Dead," "A Game of Chess," "The Fire Sermon," "Death by Water," and "What the Thunder Said." Eliot chooses, appropriately enough, to begin his poem with a section called "The Burial of the Dead," a heading that brings the remembrance of the war into the poem almost immediately. Burial of the dead is one of the most frequently repeated actions of war, and in beginning here, Eliot is taking us back into the war—almost. Burial is a finalizing action, and in this first section of the poem it takes us back only far enough to close off the war itself as material for examination, burying the war along with its dead. This section contains nearly all the traces of the war that Fussell mentions and several oblique suggestions of it that he does not. The section, for instance, displays the resentment at the promise of life continuing, at spring rains "stirring / Dull roots," at the fulfillment of the promise of renewal. Counterpointed against that is the failure to fulfill a similar promise, the "desolate and empty sea" which does not return "Mein Irisch Kind" to the hyacinth girl. (Nor should one forget, in this context, the specific German–Irish alliance of the Easter Rebellion of 1916.) The section also contains the nationalistic objection, "Bin gar keine Russin, stamm' aus Litauen, echt deutsch,"

and an almost prelapsarian Germanic innocence. It is in this
section, too, that we first encounter the "Unreal City":

> Under the brown fog of a winter dawn,
> A crowd flowed over London Bridge, so many,
> I had not thought death had undone so many.
>
> (11.60–63)

Eliot is speaking here of the dead souls among the living as
well as the actual dead returning to the city. Frye notes, of
this passage, that the subway from which the crowd emerges
is appropriate to the original context in Dante, but the use
Eliot makes of Dante is more complex than a simple pairing
of situations. Even Anne Wright, who elsewhere insists upon
the Great War as a major source for the malaise of the poem,
here attributes the line to Eliot's burial in "dull office routine"
at Lloyd's Bank.[9] It seems equally plausible that both the
tube-station (if that is where the crowd is coming from) and
the original passage in Dante are appropriate to the moment
because they evoke two images the war impressed on the
modern consciousness: the mass grave and the trenches. The
spiritually dead, then, find counterparts not only in the sub-
terranean world of the Inferno but also in the physically dead
of the recent war. Here again, the causes, it seems, are simply
données; it is the wrestling with effects that occupies the
poet.

"A Game of Chess" is the most clearly war-related section,
for a number of reasons. First of all, chess is a war game,
requiring strategy and the capture (killing) of pieces. Within
the section, however, is an even more direct reference to the
military, to Albert, who has been in the Army four years, and
within that passage is a telling statement on the results of
the war:

> He's been in the army four years, he wants a good time,
> And if you don't give it him, there's others will, I said.
> Oh is there, she said. Something o' that, I said.
>
> (ll.147–149)

The reason, of course, that there are so many who will offer Albert a good time is that wholesale deaths of young men have created a huge surplus of unattached women. What appears at first, therefore, to be a sordid, isolated scene contrasted against a remembered ideal of love takes on more universal, poignant overtones as a reminder of the thousands upon thousands of dead young men, lost in the war, and of the equally numerous situations of which this dialogue is typical.

The remaining three sections, while still concerned with images of death and destruction, are less closely tied to the Great War itself. They do, however, reinforce the more general themes, and the tangentiality of their references to the war serves to integrate it into the broader state of culture with which the poem struggles. The war is a critical moment in modern consciousness for Eliot but by no means the only one. The muting of references serves to blend it into the whole of experience, to make it always loom in the background. In the poem itself, the death and destruction themes are carried to greater lengths, and in fact they become the death of European culture and spiritual life. The downfall of civilization that Eliot describes is due, in large part, to economic factors, as the "Death by Water" section shows:

Phlebas the Phoenician, a fortnight dead,
Forgot the cry of gulls, and the deep sea swell
And the profit and the loss.

(11.312–314)

Frye sees Phlebas' death as accompanied by a cyclical rebirth[10] that is virtually required if one sees the poem as conditioned by a reading of Weston and Frazer. The resentment at renewal and the actual failure of renewal and return in the poem's first section suggests a similar rift in the case of Phlebas. There seem to be few instances in the poem to support Frye's optimism, for while Eliot draws extensively on Weston's work, he also inverts much that he finds there.

Indeed, much of the poem can be taken as an inversion of earlier forms of poetry and romance. For instance, the opening takes the sweet showers of *The Canterbury Tales* and turns them into "April is the cruelest month." There are no sweet showers in this poem. Rain brings not the promise but rather the threat of life, and this inversion of imagery baffles those who, like Frye, attempt a purely archetypal reading:

> Poets tend to identify, by metaphor, the different aspects of cyclical movement in nature. Winter, death or old age, night, ruins and the sea have ready-made associations with each other, and so have spring, youth or birth, dawn, the city, and rain or fountains. Eliot's fondness for cyclical imagery meets us at every turn.[11]

Eliot's fondness, however, does not preclude the possibility of his turning that cyclical imagery back against itself. Look for a moment at the second grouping in the previous excerpt; all of those images are associated with fertility and life. In the poem, on the other hand, they are associated with the first group of images: spring is cruel, the city is dead, the rains fail, and birth has no place. The cycle Frye sees as a necessary component of the poem does not follow so neatly as he would have the reader believe, because the two associative groups do not balance each other out. While the poet does draw heavily on the Grail legend, he inverts much that he finds there to suit his design, for he does not find the Grail in *The Waste Land.* An inversion of the death-by-drowning motif from a purifying experience to a nullification is not surprising within the context of the poem.

Just as Phlebas is killed for his commercial interests, so the death of Europe is associated with the avarice and the commercialism it displays. In what stands as virtually the only idyllic moment of the poem, the sounds of the mandolin and the fishmen's chatter, Eliot shows a rare glimpse of the "real" city untainted by the large commercial interests that have made it unreal. This pleasant moment is sandwiched between two ugly images, the encounter between the typist and the "small house agent's clerk," who is associated with Bradford manufacturing wealth, and the Thames, disgustingly filthy from its use by commerce. The loss of pastoral innocence and the rise of technological capitalism are linked closely in the poem, and the destruction of the unreal, pan-European, dead metropolis is brought about by an economic war. Historically, the environment of crumbling empires and self-serving alliances of the participants in the war suggests a decay that precedes the war itself, so that the conflict, seen by Germany as its only viable economic alternative, is perhaps not so much cause as symptom, delivering the fatal shock to an already dying organism.[12]

A second connection with the war and the death of Europe is in the figures of the hooded horde swarming. There are three related images at work here: the cicada, the swarming horde, and the mysterious third hooded figure of lines 360–366. The cicada, or locust or grasshopper (the precise insect described by these three names varies with locality), traditionally has been associated with plagues, bringing death and starvation in its attack. It becomes an apt image for the poem because it is a swarming insect and because its general outline is of a hooded figure. The hooded horde swarming, then, may be representative of Christ walking with the disciples to Emmaus (suggested by the mysterious third figure), but it may also be the plague, the army of swarming locusts descending on the already barren land. The image of armies brings with it yet another remembrance of the war. Wright links it, moreover, with line 373, "Cracks and reforms and bursts in the violet air," which "carries an aural and visual association with a bombing raid. . . . [and] is an oblique rendering of the war." Certainly the line suggests bombs and shells exploding, and the phrase "violet air" conjures up, if momentarily, "violent air" in the reader's mind. While the passage is not an overt war scene (just as there are no overt Lloyd's Bank scenes, nothing to pin down the focal point of all this angst), it pulls us in several directions, one of which assuredly must be the memory of the recently completed war.

Yet another connection lies in the thunder of section five. The thunder is not that promising regenerative powers of rain, but "dry sterile thunder without rain." Such a description, coupled with the equally sterile and dry landscape of the passage and the "hooded hordes swarming / Over end-less plains," indicates not thunder at all, but the thunder of guns, as an echo. The thunder as weapon also leads rather logically into the falling towers of the composite Eurasian city of lines 374–377.

A fairly common reading of the poem suggests that death is brought to the wasteland, Europe, and that the poem is a funeral service for the dead civilization. The movement of the poem would seem to corroborate such a suggestion, begin-ning with the Anglican burial service and ending with a ben-ediction of peace. The greater misfortune, however, is not that Europe is dead and dying, but that the death is irrevo-cable and, in a sense, retroactive, pulling the past down with the present. A pair of images come to mind to support such a sense. One is the twin figure of Elizabeth and Leicester, who are merely another example of life failing to come to fruition (and whose proximity to the typist and the clerk is telling). The other is "O O O O that Shakespeherian Rag" in which the glories of the master poet are demeaned by tawdry jazz-age tongues. Infertility at all levels—natural, human, spiritual, and cultural—becomes the central problem for which the wasteland image stands. Much of that fertility has been lost in consequence of the war: the human, of course, but also the natural and the cultural, through the terrible de-struction of the shelling, the "dry sterile thunder." And of course the war, as the poem suggests, did destroy the past, particularly the architecture and statuary of the past, with which it came into contact.

The infertility on which the poem focuses much of its at-tention, and which leads to the imagery of the Grail legend, has in a sense created its own kind of criticism. There is no doubt that Eliot has the Fisher King and the Grail images, among others of dying and reviving gods and lost and recov-ered fertility, in mind. These connected images have led a number of critics to see the poem, as Frye does, as a cyclical process, from the burial of the opening to the regenerative rains of the close. Such a reading is attractive but not entirely accurate.

Here again, Eliot subverts the traditional cycle, turns it from ritual into grotesque rather than romance:

That corpse you planted last year in the garden,
Has it begun to sprout? Will it bloom this year?

(11.71–72)

This reference to ritual death of fertility gods is twisted and blown out of proportion; the poet suggests the citizens of the unreal city have corpses in their gardens, and that those corpses are not gods who will revive but common cadavers that will decay and return to nature as humus. The problem with either possibility is that it does not fit the larger context of the poem. The image of fertility presented in those two lines is therefore ironic, as their tone implies, and the "corpse you planted" will not sprout at all. The counterpointing of mythic with modern is the more poignant because, unlike the mythological fertility gods, the young, virile men killed in World War I can never be revived nor will they help to continue the species. The dead do not regenerate in the modern world.

That dying and reviving god imagery gives way in section five to the hooded figure, the image suggestive of the crucified and resurrected Christ walking with the two disciples to Emmaus. The ironic counterpointing of the earlier instances of reviving gods turns against itself at this point in the poem because it finds in this Christ figure not a promise but a threat. The context in which the hooded figure appears, that of the swarming horde and the cicada and the drought, lends a frightening ominousness to the already mysterious figure who is never actually identified by the poet. That the possible presence of the resurrected Christ offers no comfort finds support in other of Eliot's poems, from "Christ the tiger" in "Gerontion" to an ambivalence at the birth of Christ in "Journey of the Magi," with its "I should be glad of another death." As with the fulfillment of the natural cycle in the poem's opening, this renewal provides a bitter contrast to the condition of the merely human elements of *The Waste Land*. Yet, the mere possibility of a traditionally Christian resolution remains a tantalizing alternative for many readers of the poem, despite, as Eloise Knapp Hay discusses in *T. S. Eliot's Negative Way,* the absence of textual corroboration:

> Nowhere in the poem can one find convincing allusions to *any* existence in another world, much less to St. Augustine's vision of the interpenetration between the City of God and the City of Man in *this* world. How then, can one take seriously attempts to find in this poem any such quest for eternal life as the Grail legend would have to provide if it were a continuous motif—even a sardonic one? [13]

The answer lies in the "teasing openness," as Wright calls it, the very absence of "a coherent center," in Davidson's phrasing, in which traces of various cultural patterns and modes of thought and belief are either obliquely present or drawn forth from the reader, whom Eliot treats as a willing accomplice in the creation of meaning. This is a poem of absences; reading it becomes an exercise in understanding what is not there.

Both the impotence of society and the crumbling tradition are realized in the single image of the ruined or falling tower. The tower in a state of decay is a common symbol for the decay of society, and appears in the work of Yeats at nearly the same time as *The Waste Land,* although with a major difference: Yeats restores his broken tower, both in his poetry and in his life. In the wasteland a broken tower cannot be restored; it remains to another poem, *Ash-Wednesday,* written some eight years later, for an ascent up the stairs to appear. As an image of a crumbling phallic symbol, the ruined tower also serves as a final image of impotence and infertility in the poem: "Le Prince d'Aquitaine a la tour abolie" (1.430), an image of the male inability to regenerate.

Eliot does in fact picture the people in his wasteland as unable to regenerate. There is the reminder by Lou the charwoman that the fertile men will not all be returning from the war. At the same time she reveals that even those who do return, such as Albert, will be unable to father children. All the people of the postwar Waste Land are unable to regenerate either through a flaw in the male, often pictured as death, or in the female, which takes the form of lack of sexual desire or, as in the case of Lil, a desire not to procreate. Then, too, there is the image of the personality-melting that renders fertility impossible. Woman melts into woman, man into man, prophet into prophet, god into god, until the sexes begin to melt into each other and to culminate in the figure of Tiresias, perhaps the ultimate figure of infertility. He has the characteristics of both sexes, but at the same time, he is neither. He is at once beyond sex and without it, a sexless, infertile, aged voyeur.

The infertility in *The Waste Land* goes beyond the human level to a more general symbolic infertility. This inability of the land to regenerate is most explicit in the section "What the Thunder Said,"

> Here is no water but only rock
> Rock and no water and the sandy road
> The road winding above among the mountains
> Which are mountains of rock without water
> If there were water we should stop and drink
> Amongst the rock one cannot stop and think
> Sweat is dry and feet are in the sand
> If there were only water amongst the rock
> Dead mountain mouth of carious teeth that cannot spit
> Here one can neither stand nor lie nor sit
> There is not even silence in the mountains
> But only dry sterile thunder without rain.
>
> (11.331–42)

The dry, rocky landscape runs to nightmarish proportions in this passage and the one following, emphasizing the dry sterility. The arid climate runs through much of Eliot's work during and after the war, including "Gerontion" and "The Hollow Men":

> Tenants of the house,
> Thoughts of a dry brain in a dry season.
>
> ("Gerontion," 11.75–76)

and

> Or rats' feet over broken glass
> In our dry cellar.
>
> ("The Hollow Men," 11.9–10)

These other poems do not prove, of course, the failure of the rains at the end of *The Waste Land,* but they do support a contention that there is not the cause for optimism that a purely archetypal reading would lead to. There is a damp gust bringing rain at the end of the poem, although no actual rain, but even here the promise of renewal must be doubted. One is reminded of Catherine Barcley lying dead while Frederic Henry walks from the hospital in the rain that brings no spiritual rebirth and mocks the failure of the process of birth that has killed her. There is also the memory that Spring, the time for renewal, was the favorite time for launching offensives,[14] and that the rains at Passchendaele brought not regeneration but death to the soldiers who drowned in the mud.[15] While it is impossible to carry metaphors from one author to another, it is interesting to note that the regenerative rains fail so often in literature of the Great War, sometimes failing to come and sometimes failing when they do.

So it is finally that dryness and sterility rule *The Waste Land,* a land of infertility in which the planted corpse will not sprout and the dead tree can give no shelter. Perhaps it is in this context that the poem as funeral service makes the most sense. The city is itself planted, the tower in ruins, and while it may be that, as Kenner claims, "Cities are built out of the ruins of previous cities, as *The Waste Land* is built out of the remains of older poems,"[16] it may also be that, in the infertile world Eliot presents, the ruins of civilization cannot regenerate at all. Calling the poem "an expression of horror at the panorama of anarchy and futility within the poet's mind as well as outside in the modern world," Hay notes, "The poem's nightmare vision of Europe after the Peace Treaty of Versailles helps to explain why no Western formula for peace could satisfy Eliot at the time."[17] It may be that the war-ruined culture can only hope for the specifically Eastern shantih of the benediction.

Indeed, the prospects for the peaceful society are little better, as "The Hollow Men" shows. They are explicitly not products of the war:

> Remember us—if at all—not as lost
> Violent souls, but only
> As the hollow men
> The stuffed men.
>
> (11.15–18)

They are products of peace and yet like their wartime counterparts of *The Waste Land* in their lack of spiritual substance. A major difference between the two poems is that the emphasis of the later work is not so much on the failure to regenerate as on the lack of anything to be regenerated. The landscape is much like that of the longer poem, a dead, barren land, a cactus land, a landscape suggesting both emptiness and infertility. So the hollow men are empty and infertile, perhaps infertile because empty. There is also much in the imagery of the poem that recalls the earlier poem, from the rats and the hollow valley to the falling of the Shadow, the threat, again, of a vaguely seen figure. There is nothing left to them but meaningless ritual and "deliberate disguises," the disguises of children's games and hollow piety.[18] They practice not a sham religion but an empty one. They are the hollow men, the men without positive traits of good or evil, living a meaningless and hollow existence. Nor will the hollowness be reproduced; they are the last generation, and they know it:

> This is the way the world ends
> This is the way the world ends

This is the way the world ends
Not with a bang but a whimper.

(11.95–98)

It is not the thunder of guns that destroys their wasteland
but the quiet hollowness that simply stops with a whimper.
In a way, the hollow men are the true populace of the wasteland, impotent, pathetic, meaningless, vacuous. Their infertility, like that of the wasteland itself, may be a blessing rather
than a curse. Moreover, the peace that they inhabit, in which
they are dying, is itself a product of war. This is not a prelapsarian garden but a land ravaged and wasted, full of broken
glass and lost kingdoms.

A second difference between the two poems is that, in
"The Hollow Men," Eliot does not attempt to distance himself
from his material in the same violent way he does in *The
Waste Land*. In the earlier work, there is a sense that he is
using the past to indict the present, that he invokes the language and the monuments of a richer, more fertile time to
sharpen the contrast with the thin, sterile culture of his own.
By using these fragments of the past, he is attempting to set
his own monument among the existing order, to protect it
against the ravages of the wasteland he describes, to portray
without being tainted. Finally, though, he cannot, and he realizes in section five that he is implicated by his methods,
that his ransacking of the past is a corollary activity to "O O
O O the Shakespeherian Rag." Rather than the borrowings
protecting him from the present, they are colored by it themselves; they lose much of their original meaning and take on
meanings from the present context. Eliot realizes the failure
of his attempt, doomed to failure because of the demands it
makes on the world. And so he finishes, no longer demand-
ing that modern society measure up to past glories, but asking, "Shall I at least set my lands in order?" Even though
London Bridge is falling down, the poet must look to his own
problems, must shore the fragments not against society's
ruins but against his own.

3 / *Go Down, Moses,* History, and Narrative Form

The present of *Go Down, Moses* is steeped in the past. Indeed, the narrative present frequently is the past, as the various stories move backward and forward in time with a fluidity that belies the stability of the present, even of the reader's own apparently stable present. The reader is drawn into and thoroughly enmeshed in an entanglement of generation, race, personal and public history, blood ties and prejudices, and wilderness that seems to have existed before time and may return after it, or outside it. Time here is a far cry from Quentin Compson's petty notion of the steady accumulation of seconds, minutes, and hours toward death that makes him break his watch. The past coexists with the present (Carothers McCaslin walks around with Isaac McCaslin and Carothers Edmonds and Lucas Beauchamp as much as they walk with each other), and the future often seems available as well (as when Sam Fathers and Ike "see" the future of the wilderness tied up with their own future, implicit in the moment).[1] The impulse to tell a simple, clear story of the present is over-

---

Adapted from "History, Private Consciousness, and Narrative Form in *Go Down, Moses,*" by Thomas C. Foster, from *Centennial Review* (Winter, 1984). © 1984 by *Centennial Review.* Reprinted with permission.

whelmed by hordes of images and specters from the past, so that the most casual narrative becomes a major detour through qualifications, clarifications, recapitulations, genealogies, and relationships.

Those entanglements of the text are an attempt to find a satisfactory form for dealing with the economic, racial, familial entanglements of the South, which he distills into the history of a single family, itself not greatly worse, indeed perhaps more enlightened, than the average. While the story is local, its implications are vast, as are the cultural forces at work, forces of such a magnitude that even Faulkner himself, while recognizing the hazards, is not immune. As Thadious Davis notes, he is unable to free himself fully of the cultural stereotype of the black Southerner, although he sees it clearly enough to employ it as much of the source of the dramatic problem. Perhaps that is why, then, the novel offers

> no clear resolutions to the compounded tensions of the work: hidden crimes against blood kin, legacies of slavery and injustice, rape of the virgin land, father-child conflicts, the passing of the old way of life. While these problems are not resolved, there is an uneasy truce at the end, a recognition that the individuals of the community cannot strip themselves of their collective guilt or interdependency, but they can act according to the old verities of the human heart.[2]

If Faulkner can offer no clear resolution—and neither Ike's encounter with Roth's mistress nor the exchange between Molly, Miss Worsham, and the befuddled Gavin Stevens suggests he can—he is certainly capable of indicating the extent of the difficulty. The structure of the novel, coming as it does shortly after *Absalom, Absalom!*, which Davis calls "the artistic culmination of Faulkner's most creative period" (239), represents his wrestling with the problems that confront the South in formal as well as thematic terms. In confronting a situation in which nothing is fixed or safe, where the certainties implicit in linear narrative do not obtain, the novelist hits upon an interrupted form as a solution.

Nor is this true only at the level of whole stories; even at the most elemental level of narrative, the sentence, the same pattern can be discerned: sentences begin, apparently simple and declarative, only to be inundated by clauses and phrases that modify, reduce, expand, clarify, or subvert the initial meaning as the past rushes in on that meaning. The informing principle of *Go Down, Moses* exerts its influence outward beyond the level of story to novel (despite arguments, possibly valid in other contexts, that the book is not cohesive)[4] and inward to a single syntactic unit, reinforcing and highlighting the larger narrative.

The book opens with a pair of such sentences, if indeed the second can be called a sentence:

> Isaac McCaslin, 'Uncle Ike', past seventy and nearer eighty than he ever corroborated any more, a widower now and uncle to half a county and father to no one this was not something participated in or even seen by himself, but by his elder cousin, McCaslin Edmonds, grandson of Isaac's father's sister and so descended by the distaff, yet notwithstanding the inheritor, and in his time the bequestor, of that which some had thought then and some still thought should have been Isaac's, since his was the name in which the title to the land had first been granted from the Indian patent and which some of the descendants of his father's slaves still bore in the land.[5]

This sentence contains a great deal of apparently needless information, one way or another, and still more of it as the second sentence goes on. Why, for instance, is it important to know Edmonds' relationship to Ike? Why even is Ike needed at all at this juncture, when he will make no direct appearance until the fourth story? The second sentence, in its second paragraph, moves toward something like an answer:

> not something he had participated in or even remembered except from the hearing, the listening, come to him through and from his cousin McCaslin born in 1850 and sixteen years his senior and hence, his own father being near seventy when Isaac, an only child, was born, rather his brother than cousin and rather his father than either, out of the old time, the old days. (4)

The story that follows will predate Ike by several years, and yet it has importance for him, enough so that it sticks with him from a mere retelling. Its significance to him is twofold: it gives him a picture of his father to supplement the few he has from personal recollection, and it provides him with a connection to "the old time, the old days." Its significance for the reader goes beyond this to give us an insight into Ike and his background, particularly when teamed with the diary entries in "The Bear," into the automatic, although unmalicious, indifference of his culture to the black man. However, such a significance does not explain the relationship of part one to the rest of the story—nor can it ever, for read backward from the story, part one must necessarily seem out of place, inconsistent. Rather, "Was" must be read from part one forward toward the rest of the book, so that it, along with the two stories that follow, form a parenthetical insertion in the narrative of Isaac McCaslin. (Ike's appearance resembles that of the protagonist of Greek drama and reminds us the term proto-agon [first actor] refers to the hero, who normally appeared on stage first.)

Within that parenthesis are three stories about the world, past and present, in which Ike lives. None of the stories mentions him as a participant or a direct force with the exception of Lucas Beauchamp's belief that he was hustled out of his inheritance and that the Edmonds family therefore is a usurper wrongfully occupying the McCaslin farm. "Pantaloon in Black" does not mention him at all, yet it seems to have a legitimate claim to its place in the book, as do the others. This rightful place, however, can only be explained (if the book is to be seen as having unity) if the stories are read as background—important in their own right but background to the larger context nevertheless—in parenthesis. The idea of parenthesis, of discontinuation for the purpose of providing additional information, suggests itself from the uncompleted frame-tale form of "Was," which breaks in midsentence to open out on the story, never to come back to the sentence. Since the sentence is never concluded in the novel, it would be possible to say that the whole book serves to describe Ike's world, or that it all is background leading up to his socially conditioned response to Roth's part-black mistress, "Maybe in a thousand or two thousand years in America, he thought. But not now! Not now! He cried, not loud, in a voice of amazement, pity, and outrage: 'You're a nigger!'" (361). But it is more fruitful to see the parenthesis about Ike ending with his appearance proper, in "The Old People." The periodic repetition in "The Fire and the Hearth" of the book's opening reinforces such a reading by constantly reminding the reader of Ike's centrality. Interestingly, as Carl Rollyson suggests, while Ike is not present in the story, his mirror opposite, Lucas Beauchamp, is. Lucas and Ike follow contrary paths regarding respectability, society, assertiveness, and materialism, and even look to different pasts for their behavioral models, Ike to the black and Indian kings of Sam Fathers' ancestry, Lucas to the propertied white past of Lucius Quintus Carothers McCaslin.[6] Without Ike, one must recall, the conflict between Lucas and Roth would not exist, for Lucas sees Roth as the usurper of the land

> relinquished, repudiated even, by its true heir (Isaac, 'Uncle Ike,' childless, a widower now, living in his dead wife's house the title to which he likewise declined to assume, born into his father's old age and himself born old and became steadily younger and younger until, past seventy himself and at least that many years nearer eighty than he ever admitted any more, he had acquired something of a young boy's high and selfless innocence) . . . (106)

In this case the secondary information appears in literal rather than figurative parenthesis, and it reiterates the form as well as the substance of the opening, almost as if those two initial sentences were reappearing, reexerting their domination over the background material, reminding the reader that this, after all, is Ike's novel.

"Pantaloon in Black" carries no such reminder and, on first glance, is the most problematic piece in the book. Literal-minded readers such as John Pilkington find little justification for its inclusion, "Perhaps the best conjecture is that Faulkner may have decided that the moving account of Rider's suffering was too pertinent to the general racial theme to discard the story."[7] Indeed, it bears no immediate relationship to Ike and seems wholly unrelated unless read, like the first two, as background, essential to an understanding of the land and, therefore, of the man. The story-chapter's inclusion, if not immediately logical, works along more typically poetic Modernist lines, in which the juxtaposition of disparate or fragmentary elements takes on resonance and meaning precisely because of the jarring effect produced. The overall unity, moreover, is no less for the disparate elements than that of Dos Passos' *U.S.A.*, with its Camera Eye and Biography segments, against which no one ever lodges the charge that it is not a novel. If the first two stories point to the white man's blindness toward the humanity of the black, this one is a study of that humanity in all its frailty. Rider's prodigious stature only serves, by comparison, to amplify his fragility. What he tries to do is forget his humanity, to become a "nigger," and he performs all the acts expected by the culture of one. His grief, however, drives him beyond the limits of that role, one of which is that "niggers" do not kill white men even when a "man" would or when a black would be allowed to kill another black. Although he tries to put his manhood in the past and assume the identity of his race, the past keeps seeking him out:

> But it was not his knees on the floor, it was his feet. And for a space he could hear her feet too on the planks of the hall behind him and her voice crying after him from the door: "Spoot! Spoot!"—crying after him across the moon-dappled yard the name he had gone by in his childhood and adolescence, before the men he worked with and the bright dark nameless women he had taken in course and forgotten until he saw Mannie that day and said, "Ah'm thu wid all dat," began to call him Rider. (151)

Neither he nor his aunt will let him forget that he is not a stereotype but an individual human being. His relationship with Mannie is not general or racial but individual and personal, and his aunt's use of the childhood nickname, Spoot, evokes a flood of images from his own particular past. The fluidity of time is brought to bear in that single sentence, as the present and all phases of the past rush in on Rider with unbearable simultaneity. His attempt to escape into racial anonymity drives him on toward the fatal crap game.[8]

It is as an example of the black man's humanity, then, that "Pantaloon in Black" fits as part of a unified book, enlightening not only the Ike stories but the actions of Gavin Stevens and Miss Worsham in the title story as well. Indeed, without the earlier tale of black grief to support and explain it, "Go Down, Moses" appears to present mere cartoon figures as Molly and the Worshams act out their grief ritual. The story's more immediate purpose, however, is to close out the narrative parenthesis and clear the stage for the entrance of Isaac McCaslin.

Ike does not stride onto the stage, however; he materializes out of the gray formlessness in an opening evocative of both Crane's "The Open Boat" and the Book of Genesis not as "Uncle Ike, past seventy and nearer eighty than he ever corroborated any more," but as a boy shooting his first deer. The past, a rapidly dying past that will see no future of its own, pervades both "The Old People" and "The Bear," and the stories concern themselves with that past living through actors in the present. Sam Fathers passes it along to Ike in the blood ritual after the killing of the deer, and General Compson speaks of it when he tells Cass "you aint even got a good hand-hold where this boy was already an old man before you damned Sartorises and Edmondses invented farms and banks to keep yourselves from having to find out what this boy was born knowing" (250). The title, "The Old People," refers not only to the participants in the story, since it is set many years prior to the "now" of the book but also to the people of antiquity, white, red, and black, who act in the story as spirits, as presences:

> They were the white boy, marked forever, and the old dark man sired on both sides by savage kings, who had marked him, whose bloody hands had merely formally consecrated him to that which, under the man's tutelage, he had already

accepted, humbly and joyfully, with abnegation and with pride too; the hands, the touch, the first worthy blood which he had been found at last worthy to draw, joining him and the man forever, so that the man would continue to live past the boy's seventy years and then eighty years, long after the man himself had entered the earth as chiefs and kings entered it;— the child, not yet a man, whose grandfather had lived in the same country and in almost the same manner as the boy himself would grow up to live, leaving his descendants in the land in his turn as his grandfather had done, and the old man past seventy whose grandfathers had owned the land long before the white men ever saw it and who had vanished from it now with all their kind, what of blood they left behind them running now in another race and for a while even in bondage and now drawing toward the end of its alien and irrevocable course, barren, since Sam Fathers had no children. (165)

The main sentence here, "They were the white boy, marked forever, and the old dark man sired on both sides by savage kings, who had marked him" is complete in itself, grammatically, yet it says next to nothing about them or about its own meaning. It virtually requires additional information, which appears in the sentence itself: the past, the spirit of kings, lives through nature, through the buck Sam addresses, "'Oleh, Chief,' Sam said. 'Grandfather.'" Nor is it merely the white ancestry living in the boy; Sam had imparted to him the Indian and, more incidentally, the black ancestry he cannot pass along directly since he has no children. The ceremony of blood, then, is a laying on of hands, a passing on of the line of kings of which Ike, because he has no children, no one to pass the line on to, and not even a realm to pass on (the wilderness will not survive him), will be the last possessor. The sentence is wrong in this respect: "the end of its alien and irrevocable course" is not Sam Fathers but Isaac McCaslin.

The connection between Ike and the death of the wilderness is inevitable in the sentence just quoted. The main clause links them, then the first long modifying clause on the ceremony, with phrases such as "under the man's tutelage . . . joining him and the man forever, so that the man would continue to live past the boy's seventy years and then eighty years," links the two of them explicitly. The second half of the sentence then brings to the surface the ancestors of both the man and the boy in alternating dependent clauses—there are no verbs for either "the child" or "the man"—so that each clause appears as if it could be placed anywhere in the sentence, even in the main clause, in parenthesis. However, as it stands, it not only fulfills the parenthetical function of providing background and movement in time, it also reemphasizes the relationship between Sam and Ike, in form as well as content.

The connection between the two runs through all three Ike stories, even "Delta Autumn," although (or perhaps because) Sam Fathers is long dead. The connection is made through Ike's musing on the wilderness and why he never tried to save it.

> It was because there was just exactly enough of it. He seemed to see the two of them—himself and the wilderness—as coevals, his own span as a hunter, a woodsman, not contemporary with his first breath but transmitted to him, assumed by him gladly, humbly, with joy and pride, from that old Major de Spain and that old Sam Fathers who had taught him to hunt, the two spans running out together, not toward oblivion, nothingness, but into a dimension free of both time and space where once more the untreed land warped and wrung to mathematical squares of rank cotton for the frantic old-world people to turn into shells to shoot at one another, would find ample room for both—the names, the faces of the old men he had known and loved and for a little while outlived, moving again among the shades of tall unaxed trees and sightless brakes where the wild strong immortal game ran forever before the tireless belling immortal hounds, falling and rising phoenix-like to the soundless guns. (354)

His life begins not at birth and his ancestors are not the whites, or at any rate not just the whites, from whom his blood descends. Rather, life is "transmitted," given to him by Sam Fathers in his teachings and in the blood ritual as well, and by the other old people who take him to the wilderness:

Major de Spain, General Compson, McCaslin Edmonds, Walter Ewell, and even Boon Hogganbeck. This passage comes quite shortly after a recapitulation of the episode at the beginning of "The Old People," so the reader sees Ike's relationship to the wilderness revolves around not only the two men in the passage but the others as well. Moreover, shortly before that, Ike sees the human devastation of what once was the wilderness, "the land in which neon flashed past them from the little countless towns and countless shining this-year's automobiles sped past them on the broad plumb-ruled highways," and he sees the change in the men from Compson and de Spain to Will Legate and Roth Edmonds. The latter pair are figures of inheritance, Roth bearing the same given name as the progenitor of the McCaslin line and Will Legate with his curiously redundant name meaning to give by bequest; but theirs is an inheritance much diminished in stature and scope, as they themselves are diminished inheritors. The comparison shows that the wilderness life is reaching its earthly end, as is Ike.

But an earthly end is not a total cessation of existence, and the quoted passage points up a major metaphysical difference between *Go Down, Moses* and, say, *The Sound and the Fury*. In the latter work man is viewed as possessing no spiritual life, and death is therefore the end of all life; while in the former, spiritual existence is a major part of man, and life in the flesh is an imperfect stage to be suffered through on the way to the ideal state. The quoted sentence is very explicit on this point, "the two spans running out together, not toward oblivion, nothingness, but into a dimension free of both time and space." Moreover, one of those spans belongs to the wilderness that, as the reader has seen in previous stories, possesses a spiritual existence. Its relationship to Ike is, to his mind, one of contemporaries, coevals; it completes with him the process it begins with Sam. Interestingly, the two men named in this passage on the death of the wilderness are the two most closely connected with it: Sam, whose death coincides with the beginning of the end, and Major de Spain, who began selling it off to the timber company, who is in large measure responsible for turning it into "the untreed land warped and wrung to mathematical squares of rank cotton for the frantic old-world people to turn into shells to shoot at one another." The older wilderness is contrasted here with its greatly fallen successor, both of which are contrasted later in the sentence with the ideal-world wilderness. The others—Compson, Ewell, Cass, and Boon—although significant in many respects are not so closely tied to the death of the woods and therefore receive no mention here. Sam Fathers is the most important person because he symbolizes the plight of the wilderness.

If Ben is an objective correlative to the woods and his death stands for its downfall as well, then Sam is the human correlative. Similarly, the final demise has as its objective correlative "the mathematical squares of rank cotton," a complete taming of the land, and as its human correlative Isaac McCaslin, the woodsman besieged by the trappings of civilization—mistresses and city-dwellers with no respect—even as he goes out on his last trips to the no-longer wilderness. When he dies, the wilderness will be gone, and the two will move together toward a hunter's Valhalla. The structure of the sentence itself suggests freedom from earthly constraints, as it runs fluidly, relatively free of punctuation (for Faulkner), and mystical-sounding, "moving again among the shades of tall unaxed trees and sightless brakes where the wild strong immortal game ran forever before the tireless belling immortal hounds, falling and rising phoenix-like to the soundless guns." It is for this world Ike has spent his life preparing, for a world where the natural aristocracy of Sam Fathers and Old Ben and Major de Spain and General Compson dominates over lesser beings, where trappings of society are worthless (just as Ike, earlier, has to give up his compass to see the bear), where the warriors of the hunt may be killed each day to rise each evening.

Ike has been aware, almost since his first encounter with the wilderness, of its symbolic or mythic qualities, as embodied by Old Ben:

It was as if the boy had already divined what his senses and intellect had not encompassed yet: that doomed wilderness

> whose edges were being constantly and punily gnawed at by
> men with plows and axes who feared it because it was wilder-
> ness, men myriad and nameless even to one another in the
> land where the old bear had earned a name, and through
> which ran not even a mortal beast but an anachronism indom-
> itable and invincible out of an old dead time, a phantom, epit-
> ome and apotheosis of the old wild life which the little puny
> humans swarmed and hacked at in a fury of abhorrence and
> fear like pygmies about the ankles of a drowsing elephant . . .
> (193)

Ike's vision of the wilderness, both here and elsewhere in the
book, partakes of neither mind nor senses but of the mystical
side of experience that appears not to be part of the white
man's—or perhaps simply the modern man's—cognitive bag-
gage. General Compson, although not fully understanding
for his own part, must translate Ike's inarticulate desire to
remain in camp for Cass, who as an Edmonds, that family of
farmers and bankers—of new people—can no longer recognize his visionary side. Ike's vision allows him to break
through barriers himself, to recognize connections between
the bear and the wilderness, between black, red, and white
races, between past, present, and future, although, because
of its private quality, he cannot effectively communicate it, try
as he may in the fourth section of "The Bear." His youthful
view of the wilderness in the passage corresponds closely to
his vision of his own relationship to it in the passage quoted
earlier from "Delta Autumn," in that both are nonintellectual,
nonsensory perceptions on the intuitive, instinctive level that
seek out (or perhaps *discover* is a better word, since it implies
less willful activity) connections.

These connections enable him to move freely in mental
time and space, and they provoke the narrative of his tale
into curious peregrinations. Ike's story is, in its most distilled
form: *He had heard about an old bear and finally got big enough to
hunt it and he hunted it four years and at last met it with a gun in
his hands and he didn't shoot* (297). The rest of the story, argua-
bly the rest of the novel, stands as a commentary on that
single most important event in his life. That event, an inaction, aptly characterizes Ike and is a keynote by which the

other incidents that purport to explain it can be measured and explained. It is the elemental core from which the story builds forward and backward and to which the narrative occasionally must return to regain its perspective. The italicized sentence, for instance, occurs not in a description of the hunt but in the midst of dialogue between Cass and Ike about family history, a discussion that moves like the narrative itself and to which we shall return. The experience with the bear, however, although the most important feature of both Ike's life and the story, is the climax of neither, and it makes new demands on both the narrative and the reader. The plot cannot merely build, as it would in a typical story, to that crescendo and then drop off. Rather, it must build around it; the episode is not at the end of the novel but at its heart. Moreover, the pattern of narration is colored not only by Ike's perceptions but also by that cultural hobgoblin, the past, that continually intrudes and forces characters and narrator alike to deal with it.

"The Bear" is perhaps Faulkner's finest attempt to capture the whole world in a single syntactic unit, a goal that, as he writes Cowley, he always seeks:

> I am telling the same story over and over, which is myself and the world. Tom Wolfe was trying to say everything, get everything, the world plus "I" or filtered through "I" or the effort of "I" to embrace the world in which he was born and walked a little while and then lay down again, into one volume. I am trying to go a step further. This I think accounts for what people call obscurity, the involved formless "style," endless sentences. I am trying to say it all in one sentence, between one Cap and one period.[9]

In the case of "The Bear," the entire story serves as a parenthetical insertion to that single italicized sentence, explaining and being explained by it. Yet the attempt is no less present in the novel as a whole nor in any of his novels, and the constant telling over and over of the same story is the authorial parallel to Quentin's attempting to define his relationship to his homeland through the reconstruction of the tale of

Thomas Sutpen. Faulkner's attempt appears motivated, as is Quentin's, by a desire to reveal the true nature of his ambivalence toward the South, a relationship as complex and difficult to explain to non-Southerners as Yeats's or Joyce's ambivalence toward Ireland is to non-Irishmen, so difficult, in fact, that a lesser artist such as Quentin finds himself reduced to crying out that he does not hate the South and his creator must surely share in part of that cry.

That ambivalence works itself out in Faulkner's narratives as a dialectical movement, of which *Go Down, Moses* is in many ways the clearest example. The movement of the narrative in the novel from particular moment to general background and back and forth parallels Ike's own desire to understand his relationship to history, to find his place in it and yet not be overwhelmed, to keep himself inviolate in the face of crushing historical guilt and power. Ike refuses to accept his inheritance as commodity, and begins to explore the process, through the ledgers, of the family's ownership. When he discovers the incest and casual cruelty brought about by the historical fact of that ownership, he is moved to praxis. Characteristically, that action is an inaction, not a move to change the system but rather an attempt to extricate himself from that system. He has the opportunity for truly meaningful action but his vision fails him at the key moment; he is still too much the product of that historical movement he seeks to escape to cede his inheritance not to Cass, or at any rate not only to Cass, but to the representative of the wronged and neglected side of the McCaslin line, Lucas Beauchamp. Ike recognizes his responsibility in seeking out Fonsiba to see that she gets her thousand dollars, but he fails to recognize also that the Beauchamp claim to the land is every bit as strong as the Edmonds claim, and stronger, if Lucas is to be believed, as Warren Beck notes: "He even speaks of his cousins the Edmonds men as woman-made, as if his descent in a male line through Tomy's Turl (Tomasina's Terrel) outweighed the preceding illegitimacy and incest."[10] Ike's attempt at dialectical thinking ultimately fails because he is still too much a product of his culture, and his knowledge and insight in the wilderness, as exemplified by not shooting Old Ben, fail him in social contexts.

Ike's failure, however, is not Faulkner's. In a letter to Malcolm A. Franklin on Independence Day, 1943, he commented on the murder of twenty blacks in Detroit on the same day a squadron of black pilots flew a successful mission at Pantelleria:

> Suppose you and me and a few others of us lived in the Congo, freed seventy-seven years ago by Ukase; of course we can't live in the same apartment hut with the black folks, nor always ride in the same car nor eat in the same restaurant, but we are free because the Great Black Father says so. Then the Congo is engaged in War with the Cameroon. At last we persuade the Great Black Father to let us fight too. You and Jim say are flyers. You have just spent the day trying to live long enough to learn how to do your part in saving the Congo. Then you come back down and are told that 20 of your people have just been killed by a mixed mob of civilians and cops at Little Poo Poo. What would you think? A change will come out of this war. If it doesn't, if the politicians and the people who run this country are not forced to make good the shibboleth they glibly talk about freedom, liberty, human rights, then you young men who live through it will have wasted your precious time, and those who don't live through it will have died in vain.[10]

Faulkner's attack against injustice and inhumanity, as this letter demonstrates, aims not only at the South but at the hypocrisy and double thinking of Washington and the North as well. He writes of the South because he knows it and because the waters of bigotry and abuse are less muddied by sham humanitarianism. Unlike Ike McCaslin, Faulkner can see the consequences of ceding the inheritance to the Edmonds family, which are that very little is changed except that matters are made worse because the Edmondses, as evidenced by Zack's treatment of Lucas and Molly and Roth's dealings with his mistress, show less compassion for their black cousins than does Ike. Faulkner uses his understanding of race relations and history to create a dialectic narrative in *Go Down, Moses*; his "world filtered through 'I'" becomes a play of past and present, which is nowhere more evident than in the fourth section of "The Bear." The section opens and closes with incompleted sentence fragments, and the remainders of those sentences are missing from the book; the effect of these fragments is to open the section out onto the preceding and following sections, so that its meaning is not intrinsically its own but belongs instead to the rest of the story. Moreover, despite the use of a number of periods and question marks, the customary indicators of completed sentences, the section stands as a single syntactic unit, a continuous, flowing, unbroken, parenthetical insertion that just happens to be sixty-one pages long. This substory, in true dialectical fashion, has no justification of its own but finds its justification in the main story, on which it acts in turn, not as background but as process of Ike's discovery of self in history. His discovery of the nature of his family's ownership of the land and his repudiation of his birthright are built on—and clarify—his earlier understanding of the wilderness and the validity of the Ikkemotubbe-Sutpen-de Spain-lumber company claims to ownership.

Similarly, the older narrative, the ledgers, with which Faulkner shares the fourth section, performs as more than mere background, becoming instead an active force in Ike's conception of himself:

> he seemed to see her actually walking into the icy creek on that Christmas day six months before her daughter's and her lover's (Her first lover's he thought. Her first) child was born, solitary, inflexible, griefless, ceremonial, in formal and succinct repudiation of grief and despair who had already had to repudiate belief and hope that was all. He would never need look at the ledgers again nor did he; the yellowed pages in their fading and implacable succession were as much a part of his consciousness and would remain so forever, as the fact of his own nativity: Tennie Beauchamp 21yrs Won by Amodeus McCaslin from Hubert Beauchamp Esqre Possible Strait against three Treys in sigt Not called 1859 Marrid to Tomy's Turl 1859. (271)

Ike not only employs the records as part of his own consciousness, he becomes an active participant in them by updating
the entry for Tennie's Jim. What Ike never seems to realize,
though, is that these records, functioning as the family Bible
for the black McCaslins, are financial ledgers, emblematic of
the single most monstrous fact of their treatment by the white
McCaslins, and from which all the other indignities spring.
He seems able to recognize and willing to atone for all the
evil in the ledgers except for the sheer fact of their existence,
which he apparently never questions. The tale told in the
ledgers acts positively on Ike, influencing his decisions
within the larger narrative. So too it acts on the readers, influencing our understanding of Ike, his noble qualities, and
his shortcomings. Moreover, the seemingly benign records
are colored by the larger narrative, as we discover with Ike,
and even beyond Ike (as in the title story) the often tragic
consequences of the events recounted in the ledgers. Then,
too, the fourth section draws together not only the rest of the
story but the rest of the novel, as it prepares us for Ike's failure to accept Roth's mistress in "Delta Autumn," a rejection
conditioned by his personal inability to recognize his historically dictated response to blacks not as people but as chattel.

The final section of "The Bear" reminds us that Ike's place
is, after all, in the woods. Just as the encounter with the wilderness brings out excellence, albeit momentary, in Boon
Hogganbeck, so in Ike it inspires a nobility and a holiness
that, despite his emulation of the Great Carpenter, fails him
in the wilderness of social contexts and race relations. Small
wonder, then, that he gives Roth's mistress a stock social response on discovering that she is black. Indeed, the response
seems to be more on the level of what society is saying collec-
tively than of a personal outcry, as he thinks, "Maybe in a
thousand or two thousand years in America . . . But not now!
Not now!" (361). It is and is not a personal response, a voice
from somewhere else that nevertheless speaks for the actor,
in much the same way nonhuman voices speak for Aziz at
the end of E. M. Forster's *Passage to India:* "But the horses
didn't want it . . . they said in their hundred voices, 'No, not
yet,' and the sky said No, not there."[12] Ike is simply too little

the social man to transfer his woods-wisdom to other contexts, and however much the final story valorizes, rightly, the response he fails to make, the response Miss Worsham does make, it can never hold him responsible in a world he has never occupied with his real living self. His recognition of the inadequacy of man's heritage and properties, human constructs both, in the face of the larger truth of the wilderness cannot carry him through the tangle of social relationships; even his relationship with Sam Fathers, close as it is, stems from the wilderness rather than from civilization, and while it represents a movement, it is not an arrival.

Indeed, Ike's failure to fully understand his relationship and responsibility to his black cousins causes the action of the title story; the executed man, Samuel Beauchamp, grandson of Lucas and Molly and the fifth generation (like Roth) from old Carothers McCaslin, was initially thrown off the McCaslin farm for breaking into a storehouse to which he held an equally strong moral claim as that of the legal owner, Roth Edmonds, and a claim he could have exercised if only Ike's liberation had been more complete.[13] Those critics who, with John Pilkington, complain that the title has only the most tangential relationship to the story because all the principals were born after the Emancipation[14] fail to see that slavery did not end on January 1, 1863, and that the "Let my people go" of Exodus and the spiritual named in the title refer to a contemporary lack of freedom that legal manumission failed to correct. Ike bears as much responsibility as Roth for selling Molly's Benjamin into Egypt. Ike, entangled as he is in the past, functions, then, not as a model but as a bridge to that more complete liberation of the human spirit represented by Miss Worsham.

4 / *Ulysses* and Joyce's Grammar of Social Experience

Understanding Modernist literature as the arbitrary ordering of chaos has by now become a hackneyed part of the critical liturgy. And nowhere, perhaps, is this commonplace more common than in discussions of James Joyce's work, which has often been read as if Joyce were investing the essentially chaotic and meaningless flux of existence with an arbitrary mythic significance. Indeed, he seems, especially in the later novels, to invite such readings.[1] There is, however, another way of viewing the order running through the chaos, that Joyce has not put it there but found it there. His fictional characters are themselves creators of fictions: perceiving, ordering, interpreting, and acting out experience through a complex system of symbols and patterns. Nor do they arbitrarily invest experience with the power of this system, which draws its strength from the whole of Western culture and history. In his fiction, then, Joyce displays the presence of the system in his characters: in the trivial, the routine, the mundane, the scatological, the daily (and nightly) actions, they

Adapted from "Joyce's Grammar of Experience" by Thomas C. Foster. *Éire-Ireland*, Winter, 1982. Reprinted with permission from *Éire-Ireland*, St. Paul, Minnesota.

express themselves through the system, which veers increasingly toward a complete language of symbols or archetypes as his work matures. In *Dubliners*, the sense of cultural system is limited to individual characters' relationships with their personal (or, as in the case of Parnell, the immediate historical) dead; in *A Portrait of the Artist as a Young Man*, the emphasis is still on an individual, Stephen Dedalus, but he brings to bear on his experience an increasingly broad sense of history and culture; in *Ulysses*, both the patterns and their expression become collective as well as individual, as the system takes on properties of language; whereas, in *Finnegans Wake*, the individual is all but lost under this "language of archetype."

It is in *Ulysses* that the interplay between the individual and society achieves its fullest development. At the end of the *Portrait*, Stephen has withdrawn from Dublin, from the world of contingency and flux, because it fails to conform to the set of images he employs to understand it. So he goes to Paris, hoping for an ideal world.

In *Ulysses*, he returns to that world of contingency and flux, for the ideal world ultimately is untenable. The world of contingency, however, is problematic for character and author alike, and Joyce's portrayal of this world has led critics to read the book as the superimposition of order on chaos. Indeed, many have found the order as chaotic as the raw material, so much so that Stanley Sultan, viewing the critical shambles of forty years, feels compelled to return to the book's *argument*, to begin *Ulysses* studies again with plot analyses.[2] These readings of order over chaos, however, allow for only two interpretations, both unsatisfactory: Joyce is elevating the characters to mythic and universal levels and their earthly existence is mere formality, to be ignored; or else, Joyce constructs the mythic framework as a large scale framework against which his paltry characters can be even further diminished and degraded. Hugh Kenner, in his *Joyce's Voices*, offers the definitive discussion of the narrative nastiness of *Ulysses* in suggesting that Joyce lets the characters hang themselves, that he incorporates their words into the narration the better to ridicule them.[3] Such a reading is possible, if we read the novel, as Kenner does, as simply an extension of the narrative method of *Dubliners*. It fails to account, however, for two important points: Joyce learned from his first book that such an ungenerous narrative voice implicates the speaker as much as those spoken of and there is no excuse for a seven hundred page novel whose main purpose is to knock down straw men.

In addition to the mythic parallels, the stream-of-consciousness technique is frequently discussed as an overlay, a filter for arranging the events of Bloomsday into an orderly, manageable form.[4] These readings turn the book back in on itself, following a tendency that it displays toward insularity, so that the world of *Ulysses* has few points of contact with the world outside the novel, and those (most commonly) are autobiographical.[5] But, for many studies, even that extraliterary connection is secondary to the novel's literary or mythic parallels, so that work after work contains a version of the schema, and we are faced with an endless series of variations on Stuart Gilbert's book. The schema becomes the novel, for many critics, and the cleverness of the production overwhelms the reader's sense of the book, as Edmund Wilson complains: "It seems to me difficult, then, not to conclude that Joyce elaborated *Ulysses* too much. [The flowers in Lotus-Eaters] do not create in the Dublin streets an atmosphere of lotus-eating. . . . And do not the gigantic interpolations of the Cyclops episode defeat their object by making it impossible for us to follow the narrative?"[6] Wilson's comments, like the work of so many illuminators of *Ulysses*, are invited by Joyce, in the novel itself as well as in his handing out copies of the schema and in encouraging, if not actually supervising, Gilbert.

Such commentaries rest on the usually unstated assumption that the novel's artistic pyrotechnics exist for their own sakes, in a state of aesthetic isolation, and that they are themselves the controlling forces, the raison d'etre, of *Ulysses*. Even such fundamentally different critics as Sultan and Lukács find room for agreement:

> Their [Cervantes, and Sterne's] play was created for its own
> sake as a quality of their art; Joyce's modernist play had to be
> work as well. That is to say, his parodies, burlesques, tricks,
> and manipulations of the conventions of the novel as a genre
> are not only play that points outward to a particular writer,
> literary form, or real situation; they are also and primarily—
> like his patterns of allusion—purposeful work that functions
> within *Ulysses*.[7]

> I refer to the fact that with Joyce the stream-of-consciousness
> technique is no mere stylistic device; it is itself the formative
> principle governing the narrative pattern and the presentation
> of character. Technique here is something absolute; it is part
> and parcel of the aesthetic ambition informing *Ulysses*. With
> Thomas Mann, on the other hand, the monologue interieur is
> simply a technical device, allowing the author to explore as-
> pects of Goethe's world which would not have been otherwise
> available.[8]

Both Sultan and Lukács, then, see the technique as central to
the novel (Lukács, I believe, would go further still and say it
is the novel), and both see that technique as a purely internal,
or at least purely literary, concern. Yet, neither offers a reason
for the centrality of that technique. Lukács, of course, seeks
no answer, finding rather that the excessive concern for technique is his answer, that Joyce, like Kafka and Musil, is alien-
ated to such an extent that the Dublin he "lovingly depicts is
little more than a backcloth; it is not basic to [his] artistic intention."[9] In short, he takes the stream of consciousness as
symptomatic of the decay of art under the bourgeois. Sultan,
on the other hand, has no such ideological need to find Modernism wanting—quite the opposite, he is tremendously
positive about what he calls "Our Modern Experiment"—yet
he, too, offers no rationale for the novel's concern with technique, apparently finding it its own justification. Technique,
for Sultan as for so many Joyceans, is a purely internal matter.

Lukács objects to stream of consciousness as a formative
principle because it appears to reinforce the isolation of the
character from other people and from personal and private
history: "He does not develop through contact with the
world; he neither forms nor is formed by it."[10] This debase-

ment of character by technique he opposes to realistic fiction, in which narrative method exists to produce an understanding of character (as evidenced by his praise of Mann's use of the interior monologue). This view, although it focuses on different aspects of the problem, addresses very much the same issue as does Kenner's discussion of the narrative viciousness and Wilson's objection to overelaboration: the novel, including its characters, exists for the sake of technical narrative experiment. Such readings ultimately fall back on a notion of the design being superimposed on the material of the novel, order upon chaos, a profoundly undialectical way to read the novel. There is, however, another method of discussing the book, one that allows for a more dynamic connection between existence and design. The characters in *Ulysses* carry with them a system of patterns and archetypes through which experience is ordered, perceived, and expressed—in short, a grammar of experience—drawn from literature, religion, myth, history, politics, from the whole of Western civilization.

The system, or grammar, can be thought of as a language of symbolic action, and the terminology of linguistics presents a useful way of discussing the system. The entire system comprises the *langue*, the rules and standards for generating the speech of the characters, while their actual utterances constitute the *parole*. Like a language, this grammar of experience is acquired through the daily interactions of people with one another, and characters possess the ability to make utterances, often without realizing they have assimilated the system or even that such a system exists. They may order their experience, then, according to cultural or mythic forms while remaining unaware that they are doing so and quite ignorant, intellectually, of those forms. As with any language, of course, there are levels of awareness, from the narrative presence who is quite sensitive not only to the system but to the characters' individual permutations of it as well, down to someone such as the barfly of "Cyclops," who evidences virtually no awareness of such a system. Any single person, while possessing the rules of the language, is only capable, due to experience, education, outlook, interest, and immediate social context, of producing one set of utterances from all those possible. Molly, for instance, will never sound like Stephen nor Bloom like Gerty MacDowell. This is not to suggest, however, that their utterances are controlled completely by circumstance; there are many instances in the novel of characters manipulating the grammar to make it fit their circumstances or to make circumstances bearable. They cannot control the *langue*, the universe of possible *paroles* that exists externally to them; they can make choices about their particular utterances, although these choices (like the utterances themselves) often are made at a subconscious or preconscious level. Moreover, the reader participates in this language, just as he does in what we customarily think of as language, by interpreting and reconstituting the utterance in terms of its cultural framing of the character's action.

This relationship of the individual mind to the collective understanding, like the relationship of idiolectal variation to the whole of the language, does not dictate mass uniformity, but rather, it allows simultaneously for individual integrity and mutual communication. No two characters produce exactly the same set of utterances, and yet, because those utterances spring from the same underlying grammar, the characters understand one another and, more important, the reader can understand them as well. For instance, when Bloom says "'Wait, I'll just pay this lot.' The best plan clearly being to clear out, the remainder being clear sailing," (U 658)[11] the importance of the Homeric parallel (Bloom as sailor, paying "this lot," the rabble, and clearing out—Odysseus clears out the suitors and Bloom is aware that Molly takes lovers) resides not in Joyce's conscious use of it but in Bloom's unconscious linguistic calling-forth. Moreover, the language—not the action but the language and thought—also calls to mind a symbolically related action, Christ clearing the temple. The words Bloom chooses spring to his mind in light of the immediately preceding passage in which he thinks of Molly, of "the crux of it," of "your God a jew," of "a bite from a sheep," and of "tender Achilles." His words, then, are at once products generated through the cultural grammar and agents that produce expansion of that system, just as any expression in language, generated out of its grammar, either reinforces or expands the language.

This cultural grammar, although it can be expressed through ritual (and one has but to think of Mulligan's Black Mass), tends more often to inform language, whether word or thought, and the significant "events" of the novel are apt to be verbal rather than active. In fact, we see virtually none of the consequential relationships—Stephen's to his mother; Bloom's to Molly, Milly, Rudy, and his father; even Molly's to Boylan—directly but rather through the thoughts of the characters. For example, Stephen remembers his mother not as she was, a woman dying of cancer asking her son to pray for her, but as an image, transformed into a crab (the Cancer of the zodiac) coming after him, and as a ghastly priestess with her chalice of greenish bile and people kneeling at the rail of her bed. Even the relationship of Stephen and Bloom, which we do see, with its ritualistic catechism and communion, rests very heavily on linguistic expression of the experiential grammar. Nor are the expressions limited to the three main characters. Almost everyone in the book uses the grammar at some point to order experience, such as the scene in the cabman's stand when Parnell's resurrection is prophesied (following again his connection with Christ, already established in *Dubliners* and *Portrait*).

Moreover, not only are the characters' *paroles* generated from this grammar, but the utterances frequently help to shape the narrative. In the case of Molly's soliloquy, the utterance is the narrative, but this is merely the most obvious example. Each episode's *technic*, in fact, can be seen as a result of the workings of the minds of its characters: the catechisms of Nestor and Ithaca reflect the question-and-answer dialogues (and monologues) in which the characters engage; the dialectic of Scylla and Charybdis is a result of Stephen's back-and-forth "weaving and unweaving" (the image he calls forth is of a fictional character, Penelope, rather than a historical one, Socrates—this may be a comment on the relative force with which myth and history are ingrained on our consciousness); while the "headline" environment and mentality of the characters in the Aeolus episode gives rise to the boldface headlines of the narrative. The grammar's role in the characters' ordering and narrating of experience makes any traditional notion of a narrator or point of view inadequate in dealing with the book.

The Nausicaa episode is a case in point:

> Why have women such eyes of witchery? Gerty's were of the bluest Irish blue, set off by lustrous lashes and darkly expressive brows. Time was when those brows were not so silky-seductive. It was Madame Vera Verity, directress of the Woman Beautiful page of the Princess novelette, who had first advised her to try eyebrowleine which gave that haunting expression to the eyes, so becoming in leaders of fashion, and she never regretted it. . . . But Gerty's crowning glory was her wealth of wonderful hair. (U 349)

To read this passage as having a traditional narrator forces the reader to envision that narrator as sitting in judgment on his characters, making nasty, demeaning comments on them through his style. But such a reading poses problems: has not Joyce already discovered, in *Dubliners*, that such an ungenerous, sniping narrator is implicated by the act of describing the "scrupulous meanness" he seeks to stand above? And if, as I believe, Joyce's narrative voice moves beyond that vulgar nastiness in the marvelous final passage of "The Dead," to see him returning to it in *Ulysses* would be to suppose a wholly inexplicable regression. More appropriate is a version of the authorial presence as recorder or interpreter rather than narrator, as one who is sensitive to the characters' *paroles* because he shares in their *langue*, the larger system of which the individual utterances partake. Such a reading of Gerty's passages shows her thinking about herself and her world in language drawn from and, in turn, invoking fashion magazines and advertisements (as in this passage), dime store romances, and classical and biblical notions of beauty: "The waxen pallor of her face was almost spiritual in its ivorylike purity though her rosebud mouth was a genuine Cupid's bow, Greekly perfect" (p. 348).

Throughout the novel, characters express themselves and,

perhaps more important, think about themselves by means of this grammar, selecting bits of language that they then piece together into more or less coherent utterances. In so doing, they become creators of fictions, their thoughts and words no longer unmediated and spontaneous but rather narratives mediated (what could be less spontaneous than Gerty's description of herself?) by this experiential grammar, which acts as a filter even when the utterances are unconscious and automatic. The characters, then, become narrators of novels in which they are the main characters, novels that are not the novel Joyce is writing. When Kenner says that Wyndham Lewis "scored a near-miss in spotting traces of the kind of novel in which Dedalus and Mulligan imagine they are characters, while not noticing that such traces do not exist beyond the first episode,"[12] he scores a similar near miss; the traces do not exist because the fiction that the first episode's confrontation requires is not similarly required in other episodes. Just as one does not use the same sentence in every situation all day long, so neither does one employ the same fiction to explain every experience. The characters change their narrations as smoothly as they alter their sentences. So deeply ingrained is the ability to narrate experience vis-à-vis this grammar that it is second nature, and characters can coauthor segments. While Gerty's "narration" is individual, others, like the Cyclops and Sirens episodes, are public or collective. The style of Cyclops, for instance, presents the reader with very much the same problem as Nausicaa: how to deal with the inflated passages interspersed through the first-person narration. Again, the notion of a traditional narrator is untenable, yet if there is not one, who is responsible for the language of those passages?

Before turning to a discussion of that narrative voice, we need to look at how, and more particularly why, Joyce employs it. First of all, the mode of narration represents a truly democratic turn in the author's thinking. While dialectal variation is a key to maintaining a stratified class structure, the universality of language constitutes a basis for equality. Everyone in English-speaking societies speaks *essentially* the same language, and those differences of dialect upon which class prejudice and conflict depend are not structural but rather surface features. Similarly, the basic patterns of cultural and historical experience are shared by everyone, while the dissimilarities between, say, Stephen Dedalus and Gerty MacDowell are variations on a theme rather than differences in kind. As we frequently see in the course of the novel, the idiolectal variations of the cultural grammar do not impede mutual understanding or, in the collective episodes, collaborative narration.

The second major reason for the book's narrative voice is historical or geographical: a non-Irish Joyce would not, in all probability, have written *Ulysses*. In one of his Triestine lectures of 1907, he discusses the factors behind the paralysis of Ireland like this:

> The soul of the country is weakened by centuries of useless struggle and broken treaties, and individual initiative is paralyzed by the influence of the church, while its body is manacled by the police, the tax office, and the garrison. No one who has any self-respect stays in Ireland, but flees it as from a country that has undergone the visitation of an angered Jove. (CW 171)[13]

In short, history and culture conspire to keep Ireland subservient and incapable of action; the past paralyzes the present. This finds its way constantly into Joyce's work and its fullest development in *Ulysses*. Language is the gift (or curse) of the past to the present. Received and subsequently passed along by each generation, it influences and is shaped by the issues of the time. The cultural grammar functions in much the same way, and the past exerts its influence over the present. Control by the church, a history of conquest and occupation by foreign powers, failed heroes, lost causes, as well as the personal dead, the ghosts of their own fathers, all contribute to the system of symbol and archetype that the characters employ in organizing experience. Moreover, the Irishness of the book adds another layer of meaning to this grammar, because the symbols and patterns available to the characters, and even the language used to give them expression, stand as emblems of the very situation they so frequently are used to describe, the oppression of the Irish by foreign powers. Such a concern manifests itself in other Irish writers, perhaps most notably in the recent poetry of Seamus Heaney, in which the civil strife in Ireland is seen as someone else's war being waged by Irishmen. The technique of *Ulysses*, then, has its basis in the cultural and political history of its country: like the poetry of Yeats, it is truly national rather than blindly nationalistic.

The narratives of *Ulysses* arrange themselves roughly into two categories: the personal, in which monologue or private (and not wholly untraditional) narration predominates, and the public, in which the narrative voice becomes decentered and group collaboration abounds. Certain episodes present difficulties in classification—for example, Ithaca exhibits elements of both the public and the private—but most resolve themselves fairly clearly into one group or the other. Of the two groups the public chapters—Aeolus, Sirens, Cyclops, Wandering Rocks, Scylla and Charybdis, Oxen of the Sun, Circe, Eumaeus, and Ithaca—present the greatest difficulties in understanding, precisely because of the decentering of the narrative voice. It is with those episodes that Edmund Wilson finds greatest cause for complaint, and in them that the disparity between action and narrative mode seems the widest.

The key to those public chapters, and in many respects to the whole novel, comes not from among them but from an early, private episode, from the classroom scene in Nestor:

> —Yes, sir. And he said: Another victory like that and we are done for.
>
> That phrase the world had remembered. A dull ease of the mind. From a hill above a corpsestrewn plain a general speaking to his officers, leaned upon his spear. Any general to any officers. They lend ear. (U, 24)

What remains in the public mind is not a date or a place, not any really significant fact of battle, but a saying, a type, a cliché waiting to happen. Stephen's response is quite perceptive; it could be any general to any officers, so that history comes down to a series of hackneyed expressions from among lost events. Perhaps, though, this situation is not the catastrophe that Stephen, in his capacity as teacher, imagines it to be. What people remember is not the battle nor the political reality nor even the personality, of the speaker but a way of organizing and talking about a certain type of experience, so that one can talk about a Pyrrhic victory with the same confidence that one is understood as when one talks about a tree. That cliché is a fact of existence in much the same way the tree is: accepted, absorbed into our consciousness, automatically known. It is in this regard that the trite, the hackneyed, the clichéd discover such power in *Ulysses*, that they afford immediate, mutual recognition of ideas, situations, patterns of experience, while the original, clever expression requires additional processing. Stephen's students, while they instantly grasp the historical saying, are disconcerted by his statement that a pier is a disappointed bridge, and he, disconcerted by their responses, determines to try it again among his friends, whom he believes will value the witticism more highly. He is not, particularly in the case of Haines, totally correct in his appraisal. Not only does the phrase-become-community-property allow for communication, it also provides the basis for collaborative narration.

The first, and possibly most striking, example of the nonpersonal narrative voice appears as the boldface headlines of Aeolus. The headline of each passage, starting with "IN THE HEART OF THE HIBERNIAN METROPOLIS," provides a key, or focus, for the section that follows. The obvious suggestion, and one quite frequently made, for the existence of the headlines is that Joyce is practicing organic form, that the modern cave of the winds, the newspaper office, warrants a journalistic treatment. Of course, there can be no doubt that the headlines in the episode parallel actual newspaper headlines, but that is a treatment, not a purpose. The unasked question is why: why does Joyce employ the headlines, and how do they fit in with the rest of the episode? To see them as authorial overlay, as Joyce mimicking the people he creates, is to render them artistically indefensible on two grounds. In the first place, such a reading forces the reader to see Joyce setting up fictional straw men for the sole purpose of knocking them over, a mean and ungenerous act quite unworthy of the effort, and a practice he gives up, as we have seen, at the end of *Dubliners*. Second, and more significant, such a reading ultimately requires that the chapter be wrenched apart into the basic narrative and a superimposed, essentially unrelated superstructure. In other words, the episode's design dooms it to failure. Such a reading is therefore unsatisfactory and requires the reader to look elsewhere for explanation, to the characters themselves. Aeolus presents the first major problem in point of view in the novel, for there is no single character the reader can follow throughout the episode. While it is true that one or the other of the book's primary characters, Bloom and Stephen, hold the stage for almost the entire episode, running as it were a main character relay, the narration does not focus sufficiently strongly on them for us to explain its structure. Rather, the newspaper office, or its inhabitants, is the focal point of the narrative presence. Nearly everyone in the office is concerned, in one way or another, with the production of the paper, and they are all familiar with what a newspaper is and what functions it performs. The form of a newspaper is part of the modern experience, a fact so deeply ingrained that we take it for granted.

Small wonder, then, that the events of the episode are punctuated by boldface headlines that inflate the actual occurrences out of proportion:

WITH UNFEIGNED REGRET IT IS WE ANNOUNCE THE DISSOLUTION OF A MOST RESPECTED DUBLIN BURGESS

Hynes here too: account of the funeral probably. Thumping thump. This morning the remains of the late Mr. Patrick Dignam. Machines. Smash a man to atoms if they got him caught. (U, 118)

The headline in this case is a possible but by no means certain version of the one on Dignam's obituary. What is more, the "story" that follows has only tangential connection to the headline, offering a possible first line to the story. It is one of the few articles in the episode, moreover, that could plausibly appear in the actual paper; others, such as "CLEVER, VERY" most certainly would not. The characters organize their collective experience by means of the common grammar most readily available to them, that of the newspaper office.

A further case can be made for such a reading by looking at the actual speech produced in the episode. Stuart Gilbert states the art of Aeolus as Rhetoric,[14] but in fact an equally strong case can be made for Reportage. While that art discussed by the characters is oratory (and while they are all pleased with clever rhetorical devices), the language function they employ to discuss it is the journalist's: narrative exposition. When, for example, Professor MacHugh relates John F. Taylor's speech, he does not simply recite it, but puts in all the pertinent information of who, what, when, and where:

> The finest display of oratory I ever heard was a speech made by John F. Taylor at the college historical society. Mr. Justice Fitzgibbon, the present lord justice of appeal, had spoken and the paper under debate was an essay (new in those days), advocating the revival of the Irish tongue. . . .
>
> —It was a speech, mark you, the professor said, of a finished orator, full of courteous haughtiness and pouring in chastened diction, I do not say the vials of his wrath but pouring in the proud man's contumely upon the new movement. We were weak, therefore worthless. . . .
>
> —Taylor had come there, you must know, from a sick bed. That he had prepared his speech I do not believe for there was not even one shorthand-writer in the hall. His dark lean face had a growth of shaggy beard round it. He wore a loose neckcloth and altogether he looked (though he was not) a dying man. . . .
>
> —When Fitzgibbon's speech had ended John F. Taylor rose to reply. Briefly, as well as I can bring them to mind, his words were these. (U, 141)

Ultimately, the listeners' attention will be focused on the remembered oration; MacHugh captures and holds it by his ability to relate the story surrounding the speech itself. He presents all the pertinent facts of the case with style but without excessive detail, so that his audience is fully informed but not distracted from the central concern. The professor proves himself a capable reporter. Throughout *Ulysses*, the ability to tell a story is highly prized, but here even more than in other episodes that talent is not only valued but actually required. A man's importance in the newspaper office extends as far as his ability to hold the center stage as a storyteller, and so Bloom is ignored and Stephen esteemed. Bloom is even cursed when his telephone call interferes with Miles Crawford's story, "—Tell him to go to hell, the editor said promptly. X is Burke's public-house, see?" (U, 137), when as editor, Crawford should be more interested in generating business than recounting an old story. And, finally, Stephen's story is not complete until he gives it a title, a headline. In such an environment, with such a common grammar, the headlines generate themselves; they grow out of the action and the characters' awareness of place.

A similar result of the grammar of place takes place in the music room of Sirens, although the phase of experience around which the characters cluster their activities and perceptions changes. Again, their thoughts cluster around a single topic, music and hearing, and indeed the episode itself, without the prefatory theme, would be explained simply enough as the jumble of thoughts while too many sensations rush in at once. But the theme is there, and it colors the rest of the scene, changing the reader's understanding of the importance of certain moments and words. Its existence can hardly be explained in purely musical terms (that is, Joyce has composed a fugue in words); since much of the theme is something less than euphonious, we must assume that Joyce could have done better had he simply wished to perform a tour de force. Rather, the creation of this fugue must be credited to the participants themselves, not to anyone. Bloom, on whom so much of the chapter is focused, has no access to certain parts, such as the opening:

Begin!

Bronze by gold, Miss Douce's head by Miss Kennedy's head, over the crossblind of the Ormond bar heard the viceregal hoofs go by, ringing steel. (U, 257)

Bloom passes outside the window a few moments later, although, for his part, he experiences scenes to which no one else has access. No single character, therefore, can produce the entire episode, and so once again the notion of a collective narration offers help in understanding the narrative structure. To return to the playing of the theme once more, of course, the characters cannot elaborate the theme prior to the experience out of which it grows, and so here it is even more important than in Aeolus to reconstitute narrative presence as an active, although noncontrolling factor. That voice is sensitive to the language of their experience—indeed, more sensitive than his characters who, while they employ (like the newspapermen) a common grammar of experience and place, probably could not recognize it as such and therefore could not reproduce it. In any such situation, there are moments, high or low points that for one reason or another register upon one's consciousness, and the narrative voice of Sirens, attentive as it is to those moments, gleans them, pieces them together, and places them at the head of the episode so that the reader will recognize the musical quality of this gathering of people who, for the most part, are not trying consciously to be musical.

In this last respect, Sirens is an apt metaphor for Joyce's own relation to the book, for in letting his characters move about and pursue their own business, yet all the while remaining sensitive to locale, to historical or geographic context, to the moment, he creates art. He certainly creates art out of even less artistic circumstances than the concert room, and a prime example would be the following episode, Cyclops. The crowd in Barney Kiernan's has nothing artistic or even genteel about it; the men are dirty, crude, coarse, nasty, and hateful. Yet here, too, Joyce finds in the individual that same relationship to history and to culture that he finds elsewhere, perhaps even stronger here than elsewhere, for these men in their frustration and bitterness are more acutely aware of the crushing weight of history and circumstance than others in the novel. The art is not in their actions but in their collective experience of those actions.

Certainly, there is little that is artistic about the conscious narrator of the episode; he is mean and ungenerous in a way the young writer of *Dubliners* never thought of being and as strongly anti-Irish (although less consciously) as he is xenophobic. He is a perfect example of Joyce's vision of Ireland debasing itself to overcome debased England:

> Out of the material and spiritual battle which has gone so hardly with her Ireland has emerged with many memories of beliefs, and with one belief—a belief in the incurable ignobility of the forces that have overcome her—and Lady Gregory . . . might add to the passage which forms her dedication, Whitman's ambiguous word for the vanquished—"Battles are lost in the spirit in which they are won." (CW, 105)

That the Irish have lowered themselves to the level of the English is nowhere as clear as in the patrons of Kiernan's pub: they have practiced hatred and bitterness toward the English for so long that they have nothing else to turn against each other. The narrator, for instance, has a bad word·for everyone and everything.

Yet the narrator and the characters do not take up the entire episode, nor even necessarily draw the reader's main attention, for there are those gigantic interpolations that have only marginal connection to the basic story:

> A most interesting discussion took place in the ancient hall of Brian O'Ciarnain's in Sraid no Bretaine Bhaeg, under the auspices of Sluagh, na h-Eireann, on the revival of ancient Gaelic sports and the importance of physical culture, as understood in ancient Greece and ancient Rome and ancient Ireland, for the development of the race. The venerable president of this noble order was in the chair and the attendance was of large dimensions. (U , 316–317)

This is very high rhetoric for the coarse and no doubt blasphemous argument it describes. The inflated language of this passage is like that of bad journalism when it moves closest to propaganda, which is probably the sort of paper, given their interest and beliefs, the patrons of the tavern most frequently read. Yet what it describes is in some measure deserving of the heightened rhetoric: the men have a very real sense that they are the inheritors of their race, that the Citizen is the modern embodiment of the ancient Celtic heroes, and that it falls upon them to reclaim the greatness of Ireland. Their combined thoughts, then, produce this understanding of themselves in terms of the ancients in language which partakes not only of yellow journalism but ancient epic as well, for it is the propaganda sheet which probably comes closer than any other modern writing form to the high language of epic.

Nor should the possibility of these men simultaneously creating this expansive rhetoric and variations of the spiteful and niggardly narration of the unnamed "I" seem surprising or out of place, since a similar phenomenon takes place in Sirens. With Simon Dedalus' song as catalyst, the characters' thoughts are focused in a common direction. They are both orchestra and audience, simultaneously producing the music and watching others produce it, with the result that, while any one or two are performing, the rest are watching and listening, so that the emphasis of the action rests not with the actors but with the viewers. And although they are overt spectators, they are unwittingly performing a music of their own. So the precedent for the simultaneous occurrence of two different and even antithetical actions on the part of the characters is established, at least in Sirens, and it is carried still further in the episode in Barney Kiernan's. It may even be that the one form of narration in Cyclops is motivated by the other, or that they both find their source in the same problem, and so they are not so antithetical after all.

To be sure, they both grow out of a nationalism that, while its manifestations are often maligned in Joyce criticism, nevertheless is quite justifiable: these men are rabidly nationalistic in a way only people who have been denied their rightful status as a nation can be—only the oppressed can fight against their oppressor. Much of the epic language, therefore, can be understood in terms of justifying the Irish claim to independence by demonstrating Ireland's past greatness and modern Ireland's position as rightful inheritor of that greatness, as with the early description of the Citizen:

He wore a long unsleeved garment of recently flayed oxhide reaching to the knees in a loose kilt and this was bound about his middle by a girdle of plaited straw and rushes. Beneath this he wore trews of deerskin, roughly stitched with gut. His nether extremities were encased in high Balbriggan buskins dyed in lichen purple, the feet being shod with brogues of salted cowhide laced with windpipe of the same beast. From his girdle hung a row of seastones which dangled at every moment of his portentous frame and on these were graven with rude yet striking art the tribal images of many Irish heroes and heroines of antiquity . . . (U , 296)

The list that follows begins with Cuchulin and works its way through such "Irish" heroes as Ben Franklin and Cleopatra, as well as some with adopted Irish first names, such as Patrick W. Shakespeare and Brian Confucius. The list is quite humorous, and even leads the reader to think of it as laughable, as something produced by the author to ridicule his characters. If, on the other hand, we see the entire passage as generated out of the characters' collective consciousness, we find that the passage fulfills several useful functions for them while retaining its humor for us. First of all, it connects these moderns to their ancestral greats and thereby lends legitimacy to their claims to nationhood. Then, too, it enhances their self-image, for the moment taking them away from their current squalor and debasement to show them their heritage, what they could have been in a free Ireland. Moreover, it suggests that they can manipulate the system for purposes of hilarity, or self-deprecation, that they can undercut their own hyperbolic rhetoric. The famous foreigners, who at first make the whole list seem ludicrous, in this context add greater legitimacy still by appearing as equals, as no greater than the Irish heroes. Quite apart from—as Wilson charges—"making it impossible to follow the narrative," this particular gigantic interpolation adds new layers of significance not only to the narrative but to the plight of the characters.

Along with nationalism comes a more than healthy dose of xenophobia for the pub's patrons. A good deal of Bloom's difficulties stem from the others' perceiving him as an outsider. They challenge his citizenship (U, 331), make much of his Hungarian ancestry, and even manage an anti-Bloom, antiforeign collaboration when he attempts to explain the hanged man's erection:

> The distinguished scientist Herr Professor Luitpold Blumen-
> duft tendered medical evidence to the effect that the instan-
> taneous fracture of the cervical vertebrae and consequent
> scission of the spinal cord would, according to the best ap-
> proved traditions of medical science . . . (U, 304–305)

Bloom is attacked on several grounds. This is a bad crowd on which to practice intellectual explanations, and he insists on resorting to the approved authorities rather than simply rid-ing with the popular wisdom. Moreover, his answers are al-ways too long for a group more interested in one-liners. In short, he simply fails to understand his audience. Worst of all, as a man whose father was not born in Ireland, he's an outsider. The collective narration turns him from an Irishman to not a Hungarian but a German, and in so doing they make him the object of their wrath for their English rulers, associ-ated in this episode as elsewhere with the Germans through the royal family. Bloom, then, is made the scapegoat for the latest version of the Germanic oppression of Ireland, and again we see the political ends accomplished through the epic heightening of the interpolation. Similarly, the anti-Semitism aimed at Bloom throughout the final portion of the episode culminates in a group narration:

> When, lo, there came about them all a great brightness and
> they beheld the chariot wherein He stood ascend to heaven.
> And they beheld Him in the chariot, clothed upon in the glory
> of the brightness, having raiment as of the sun, fair as the
> moon and terrible that for awe they durst not look upon Him.
> And there came a voice out of heaven, calling: Elijah! Elijah!
> And he answered with a main cry: Abba! Adonai! And they
> beheld Him even Him, ben Bloom Elijah, amid clouds of an-
> gels ascend to the glory of the brightness at an angle of forty-

five degrees over Donohoe's in Little Green Street like a shot off a shovel. (U, 345)

A new wrinkle is added to the collective narration in that its object, a Jew departing the scene, focuses them not only on an appropriate Old Testament incident, but appropriate Old Testament language as well. For several pages of text everyone's attention at Kiernan's has been drawn to the fact that Bloom is a Jew, first by the Citizen and then by final furious action by pointing out, quite rightly, that Christ was a Jew. This statement infuriates the Citizen who, one may presume, always considered *his* Savior an Irishman, although he, too, makes the connection, albeit unwittingly, between Bloom and Christ: "By Jesus, I'll crucify him so I will" (U, 342). Furthermore, there is, as the narrator observes, many a true word spoken in jest, or in this case ridicule, for the comparison between Bloom and the prophets, and even Christ, is apt: Bloom has come among them preaching brotherhood and love as well as peace and understanding among nations, for which he receives less than brotherly treatment.

Bloom himself picks up the link between himself, Christ, and (adding an element) Parnell—Martin Cunningham has already noted that both the Jews and the Irish are still awaiting their redeemers—in Circe, first when John Howard Parnell declares him a successor to Charles Stewart Parnell, and then throughout the sequence leading up to the litany by the Daughters of Erin:

Kidney of Bloom, pray for us

Flower of the Bath, pray for us.

Mentor of Menton, pray for us.

Canvasser for the Freeman, pray for us.

Charitable Mason, pray for us.

Wandering Soap, pray for us.

Sweets of Sin, pray for us.

Music without Words, pray for us.

Reprover of the Citizen, pray for us.

Friend of all Frillies, pray for us.

Midwife Most Merciful, pray for us.
Potato Preservative against Plague and Pestilence, pray
   for us.
(A choir of six hundred voices, conducted by Mr Vincent
O'Brien, sings the Alleluia chorus . . .) ,

(U, 498–499)

Like the characters in Cyclops and elsewhere, Bloom thinks
in terms of a savior. If, as Miles Crawford suggests, every Jew
is excited by the birth of a son at the prospect that it may be
the Messiah, then it is equally true that every Irishman is
excited by the rise of a new leader, in hope that he may be
the one to lead them to independence, the one for whom
Parnell was only a poor prefigurer. Nor is this simply a literary contrivance: the histories of Jew and Irishman—in being
denied rightful homelands, in always being subject races, in
having rights denied and revoked—are so similar that they
fairly scream to Joyce for artistic treatment despite the overt
anti-Semitism he depicts among the Irish. In Bloom both
strains come together, for his heritage is Jewish and his nation is Ireland. Small wonder, then, that Parnell and Christ
suggest in the fantasy about a ruined deliverer, for they are
both for Bloom failed saviors, prophets of some greater coming, promise without fulfillment.

The ways in which this connecting of failed saviors takes
shape present an even more interesting point of focus than
why it occurs. In Circe, the psychological drama becomes ex-
ternalized, and the form of the episode centers around performance: the drama, the Mass, Vaudeville. The grammar of
experience, never far below the surface of consciousness,
rises up in Circe, exhaustion and alcohol breaking down the
customary barrier, and projects itself out from the characters'
minds so that they witness their own mental processes without being able (as they usually are) to control them. Images
come up to them without invocation, and the mix of private,
social, historical, mythological, and ecclesiastical is thorough.
What comes through is an often absurd cluster of images, as

in the litany's references to Bloom's personal events of the day, or Stephen's encounter with his mother:

THE MOTHER

(Her face drawing nearer and nearer, sending out an ashen breath.)
Beware! *(She raises her blackened, withered right arm slowly towards Stephen's breast with outstretched fingers.)* Beware! God's hand! *(A Green crab with malignant red eyes sticks deep its grinning claws into Stephen's heart.)*

* * * *

Have mercy on Stephen, Lord, for my sake!
Inexpressible was my anguish when expiring with love, grief and agony on Mount Calvary.

(U, 582)

Stephen's manner of thinking about his mother's death has two primary sources, her cancer and her faith, and the images of her come from divergent traditions. One is the zodiac: she becomes a crab with, lest the reader miss the significance, "malignant red eyes." Throughout the novel, his images of his mother are ghastly, and they suggest that his brooding over her has moved from grief into morbidity. They also suggest the resentment that becomes more explicit in the religious images of her. The Mother's Christ-connection brings out the worst in him, his satanic *Non serviam* and his shattering of the chandelier, for in her insistence on submitting to God and Church she ceases to be simply his mother and becomes instead a representative of the forces trying to oppress him, of the nightmare he is trying to escape. It may well be that her appearance as Christ helps him dispel her image, possibly even that he casts her so that he will be able to dispel her. Whatever the causes and effects, it is clear that he thinks of her death in terms of Christ on the cross, and in his Nighttown stupor is unable to suppress that thought, so it projects out into his personal drama that, of course, the other characters do not see.

Indeed, of all the public episodes in the novel, Circe comes

closest to being private, for in breaking down the barrier between the collective consciousness and individual expression, between *langue* and *parole*, the characters temporarily
lose the ability to make comprehensible utterances and so are
lost in their private shadow plays. In this privacy they prefig-
ure Molly's sleepy soliloquy in Penelope which, as Suzette
Henke points out, prefigures *Finnegans Wake:*

> Of all the characters in *Ulysses*, Molly Bloom alone perceives
> the cyclical nature of recurrent personal history. Her soliloquy
> presages *Finnegans Wake*, a work in which Joyce moves toward
> a broader mythic perspective. In both "Penelope" and the
> Wake, Joyce posits a simultaneity of human experience. He
> conquers time and space by making all events contempo-
> raneous aspects of consciousness, accessible to the mind
> through impassioned perception.[15]

Molly, like the dreamer of the Wake freed from the constraints
of mutual intelligibility, can revel in the privacy of her utterances that, precisely because they need not communicate, are
allowed to sink into the depths of universality. In a similarly
odd way the *Wake* is at once the most individual and most
universal of Joyce's novels: as the record of a dream it deals
with the mind of one person, but that mind turns out to be
not the separate, discrete intelligence we usually imagine,
but a collective body of knowledge spanning linguistics,
literature, geography, history, and myth. Molly and the
dreamer provide both illustration and extension of revela-
tions made in the public chapters of *Ulysses*, that at our most
private level we partake of a collective, cultural grammar that
allows us to communicate with our fellow humans.

5 / Yeats's Middle Poetry and the Politics of Vision

The early poetry of William Butler Yeats manifests a naive conception of the relation between society and literature in the insistence of treating Irish subjects exclusively with Irish themes, symbols, and myths. This nationalism reveals itself not as propaganda (which he consistently battles against in his writings on the Young Ireland Poets) but as local, or perhaps national, color. His Celtic Twilight period gives us a host of Irish heroes, gods, symbols and legends, as well as rather dreamy renderings of picturesque landscapes, as in "The Lake Isle of Innisfree."

One Irish subject, however, that he rarely deals with at all is its politics. The reader of the early poems is hard pressed to discern the political and social climate of the Ireland contemporary with them. This apolitical tenor of the early poems is in part caused by Yeats's escapist tendencies, his impulse to express the here and now in terms of the there and once, so that "To Ireland in the Coming Times" is the most political poem of the early period, and only rarely does he approach social concerns that closely. However, a second, perhaps stronger, factor is at work in his poetry: his reaction against the more rabidly nationalistic poetry being produced at the same time. He seems to have intuited that jingoistic patriotism or Anglophobia was the surest way for a poet to compromise his art, to lose his soul:

> He [the artist] must make his work a part of his own journey towards beauty and truth. He must picture saint or hero, or hillside, as he sees them, not as he is expected to see them, and he must comfort himself, when others cry out against what he has seen, by remembering that no two men are alike, and that there is no "excellent beauty without strangeness."[1]

This passage points to the artistic problem Yeats wrestles with his entire career: maintaining the integrity of his individual vision while at the same time recognizing himself as part of a larger group. In this case, the problem manifests itself as the dilemma of creating a national art without losing his role as individual artist.

That dilemma leads to the seeming irony that later in his career, as he confronts Irish political and social problems with increasing regularity, he all but abandons the Irish symbols and legends characteristic of his early work. By the publication of *Responsibilities* in 1914 his poetry has begun to take on topical, even polemical dimensions. In "September 1913" the poet questions not only the present Ireland's ability to measure up to the past but also the adequacy of that past for poetically confronting the present:

> What need you, being come to sense,
> But fumble in a greasy till
> And add the halfpence to the pence
> And prayer to shivering prayer until
> You have dried the marrow from the bone?
> For men were born to pray and save:
> Romantic Ireland's dead and gone,
> It's with O'Leary in the grave.
>
>   *   *   *   *
>
> Was it for this the wild geese spread
> The grey wing upon every tide;
> For this that all that blood was shed,

For this Edward Fitzgerald died,
And Robert Emmet and Wolfe Tone,
All that delirium of the brave?
Romantic Ireland's dead and gone,
It's with O'Leary in the grave.

(CP,39)

The death of romantic Ireland becomes a statement not only on the condition of the Irish soul but on the state of Yeats's poetic as well, for if that version of the country is "dead and gone," it can no longer serve his poetry in quite the way it has before. He must therefore set about establishing a style, a symbolism, a poetic of his own that is adequate to his subject matter. It is not an easy conquest, and the resulting struggle is what Frye alludes to when he calls Yeats a "growing" rather than an "unfolding" poet:

> his technique, his ideas, his attitude to life, are in a constant state of revolution and metamorphosis. . . . Perhaps it too is a by-product of the breakdown of criticism. Dante unfolds into the *Divine Comedy* because the grammar of its symbolism is present in the culture of his time; Goethe grows into the second part of *Faust* because he has to rediscover the conventions of symbolism for himself. Yeats, then, may have been compelled to "grow" by a personal search for symbols, and if so, his revisions may signify a desire to force the developing body of his work into a single unfolding unit.[3]

Anyone who has read the early drafts of many of Yeats's poems can think of several more pressing reasons for revision than a desire to produce a unified body of poetry. Nevertheless, Frye's assertion that Yeats, finding the "grammar of symbolism" available to him unsatisfactory, pursued a continual search for personal symbols, for a coherent personal mythology to replace the failed, received mythology, is particularly evident in the work following the publication of *Responsibilities*.

One may argue with Frye's contention that this search results from the breakdown of criticism (although such a breakdown may be part of the problem), for it seems to result more from the poet's sense that the "grammar of symbolism" available to him as an Irish poet fails to give him the necessary leverage to deal with public events. If this is so, it is because he rarely treats of public events as part of the crowd, and here it is important to remember his statement that the poet "must make his work a part of his own journey towards beauty and truth." One never has the feeling about Yeats, as one sometimes may have with Eliot, that he is merely a particle of humanity as it is swept along it knows not whither. However much he is buffeted by circumstances, he always manages to absorb and reshape those circumstances into part of his own mythology, so that the poems are stamped indelibly as his production rather than his society's. Edmund Wilson's comments on prose style apply equally well to Yeats's poetry:

> The style of the seventeenth century . . . was a much more personal thing: it fitted the author like a suit of clothes and molded itself to the natural contours of his temperament and mind; one is always aware that there is a man inside, whereas with Kipling, Eliot or Shaw, the style seems to aim at the effect of an inflexible impersonal instrument specially designed to perform special functions. Yeats's prose is, however, still a garment worn in the old-fashioned personal manner with a combination of elegance and ease . . .[4]

Yeats's poetry, especially the middle and later work, comes to be very much in the nature of a garment that fits the man. Moreover, this personal mark extends beyond mere stylistic considerations; form, tone, mythology, symbolism all bear the Yeats stamp. In the case of history appearing in the poems, he usually reduces the large abstraction to a single personal experience, with the effect of making history more human, as when he reduces the colossal waste of human life that was World War I to the single tragic waste in "In Memory of Major Robert Gregory." No doubt, the special relationship of the Irish to the Great War, in which they found themselves aligned with the English, against whom they were fighting for independence, has much to do with this personalized aspect. Just as Yeats, with his Anglo-Irish background, manages to distance himself and his work from the more jingoistic brand of nationalism, so too were Irishmen, with their dislike of the English and their tradition of the "Wild Geese," able to maintain a distance from the propaganda of the British war ministry.

Yet the Yeats of 1913–1914 was scarcely prepared to deal with the host of political and nationalistic upheavals on the horizon. Thomas Parkinson notes that "the danger was very real that he could have become a poet of sentiment commemorating a personal past and a body of legend that, in "The Two Kings," was redeemed from Tennysonian reflection only by his own obsessive feeling for strangeness and the supernatural."[5] His difficulty in coming to grips with the contemporary world is compounded by his antipathy toward Anglo-American modernism, noted by Parkinson and many others and documented by Debra Journet.[6] Still, in the period from the publication of *Responsibilities* in 1914 to *The Tower* in 1928 he not only moves out of late-phase Victorianism but develops a poetry sufficiently muscular to cope with the situation in which he finds himself.

The heretofore missing element that allows him to distance himself from events and still be involved with them is the comprehensive personal mythology of *A Vision*. Throughout his career, Yeats is concerned with shaping the world as he finds it into a suitable aesthetic universe. His early attempts, as we have seen, expressions of Ireland in terms of Irish myth and legend, are naive in that he merely tries to match received tales and forms to events and situations on the basis of geography. His thinking seems to be that Irish problems demand Irish treatments, and his problems stem largely from the received nature of the treatments—an Irish handling of a literary problem is not necessarily Yeats's simply because he is Irish. The great importance of *A Vision* is twofold; it affords him a unified, comprehensive system of metaphor, symbol, and myth, and it is *his*. That *A Vision* offers him, for the first time, a symbolic network of his own, one that he at least had a hand in shaping to his own satisfaction, seems clear enough. Of equal importance is that it is also comprehensive—it gives him a totalizing system for turning personal, historical, political, and social events, the chaos of experience, into the order of art.

A Vision is at best a formidable undertaking for the casual reader, and even the scholar can hardly be expected to know the entire system by rote, although some knowledge of the phases and gyres and their application to history and personality is central to a reading of Yeats's later work. Yeats applies the actual lunar phases to man's personality traits, each phase having certain traits associated with it, while at the same time he says that the incidents, which he calls Body of Fate, in one's life are also governed by phase. On the greater scale, he asserts that history, too, is governed by lunar phase, a full cycle of twenty-eight occurring every thousand years. Two millennial cycles of twenty-eight phases each are imposed on each other antithetically, like interpenetrating cones or gyres. The gyres, as Richard Ellmann notes, are major symbols that satisfy many of Yeats's needs:

> Wedded in antagonism, they symbolize any of the opposing elements that make up existence, such as sun and moon, day and night, life and death, love and hate, man and God, man and woman, man and beast, man and his spiritual counterpart or "daimon"; on a more abstract level, they are permanence and change, the one and the many, objectivity and subjectivity, the natural and the supernatural worlds. With the gyres Yeats had a more excited and interesting picture than, for example, two armies drawn up against one another would have afforded him; for the point of one gyre was in the other's base, as if a fifth column were operating in the very headquarters of the enemy. He concurred with Hegel that every thesis had implied in it its own antithesis, and modified the notion that every movement holds the seeds of its own decay by identifying the seeds as those of a countermovement.[7]

The gyres satisfy multiple needs simultaneously for Yeats then. As Ellmann notes, they symbolize opposing elements of almost any nature, and because they are themselves moving and whirling forces rather than mere static objects, they answer the need for motion and are therefore more satisfactory as symbols for the movement of history. What in Hegel are the opposing forces working toward synthesis become in Yeats even more kinetic: antithetical gyres simultaneously whirling about a single axis, although the result is not generally so clear a synthesis. Another advantage the gyres afford is that they place the lunar phases in a larger context, an overarching structure which frees the phases from their customary relation to time so they may apply to larger spans of time without losing their essential relations to one another.[8] They offer him, in short, a personally comprehensible method of organizing history into manageable form, rather than relying on the methods of other historians.

The gyres, in their turn, are subsumed into a larger context of twelve cycles. The double millennium, which actually overruns two thousand years slightly, is the primary structure of history and is ushered in by a new annunciation of God to man. The present cycle was begun with the birth of Christ, while the previous cycle began with Zeus, as a swan, raping Leda, bringing in the Homeric period. The dozen cycles fit, more or less, into a larger cycle of 26,000 years, corresponding to the Great Year of the Ancients. A thirteenth Cycle extends the possibility of escape from the Great Wheel of history, in much the same way that it offers escape from the wheel of incarnation on the personal level. The major emphasis of *A Vision*, however, is not with escape from the process but with the process itself, with which Yeats, in the Ireland of his day, must have been constantly concerned. And so the poems that follow will be concerned with the poet's relationship, through his visionary work, with history.

With *The Wild Swans at Coole* Yeats announced a different poetry: different tone, subjects, treatment. In the title poem the evidence of change is unmistakable:

> I have looked upon those brilliant creatures,
> And now my heart is sore.

All's changed since I, hearing at twilight,
The first time on this shore,
The bell-beat of their wings above my head,
Trod with a lighter tread

Unwearied still, lover by lover,
They paddle in the cold
Companionable streams or climb the air;
Their hearts have not grown old;
Passion or conquest, wander where they will,
Attend upon them still.

                                                    (CP, 129)

This is no mere poem about a man growing older, says Yeats. "All's changed"—his fiftieth birthday, his marriage, the Great War, Major Gregory's death, the Easter Rebellion have conspired to cut off any retreat to the past, to a time when he walked "with a lighter tread." In contrast, the swans paddle "unwearied still," showing no evidence of the heaviness that burdens the speaker. Their world is just the same as it was nineteen years earlier, while his, as he sees it now, is completely overhauled. Moreover, a sense of loss rather than simple change weighs him down, as he worries over the envisioned loss of the one remaining mark of constancy, the swans themselves.

"The Wild Swans at Coole" goes beyond simply expressing loss, however, to introducing major symbols of the later poems. The swans themselves are the most immediate symbols in the poem. The final book of *A Vision* is entitled "Dove or Swan," representing the Christian and Greek cycles of history, respectively. The birds symbolize the annunciation of God (or gods) to men and usher in new ages. Of course, this does not mark the first of Yeats's bird symbolism. From his earliest poems, birds have appeared, but his infatuation with the subject matter of *A Vision* brings swans, in particular, into his poems in increasing numbers, most notably in his treatment of the Ledean myth, which, like the Christian nativity, is an active, dynamic example of the link between gods and men and, in Yeats's mind, of the beginnings of new historical eras. In "The Wild Swans at Coole," the swans have not yet taken on such full meaning, but they nevertheless represent a nonhuman world that goes on regardless of the events in the human, a world in which their hearts do not grow old with the poet's, in which passion and conquest, apparently unavailable to wearied speaker, "attend upon them still."

The second major symbol introduced in the poem is that of the gyre:

> All suddenly mount
> And scatter wheeling in great broken rings
> Upon their clamorous wings.
>
> (CP, 129)

The association with the gyres here is simply one of movement, and the reader who knows nothing of *A Vision* loses little (the same is true of the swans), for the great image remains vivid. The reader of *A Vision*, on the other hand, can see in this poem Yeats introducing symbols from the prose work as images, without forcing them to bear the symbolic load they will in the later poems. He seems to be trying to accustom the reader to the symbols themselves before introducing the ideas being symbolized, as he does again in the following poem, "In Memory of Major Robert Gregory":

> Now that we're almost settled in our house
> I'll name the friends that cannot sup with us
> Beside a fire of turf in th' ancient tower,
> And having talked to some late hour
> Climb up the narrow winding stairs to bed:
> Discoverers of forgotten truth
> Or mere companions of my youth,
> All, all are in my thoughts to-night being dead.
>
> (CP, 130)

This first stanza introduces variants of the gyres, the tower and the winding stair, which become such powerful forces in his poetry that they become titles of two later volumes. In this poem, however, they are not the major symbols they are to become but homely objects. The ancient tower is quite literally Thoor Ballylee, "our house," in which he sups beside the fire, while the winding stairs are the way to the bedrooms. The connection between the tower and stair and the gyres is not made in this poem; rather, as in the preceding poem, the objects are allowed to be themselves. The power of these later symbols, aside from their visionary functions, lies in their being local and personal objects as well. The swan is not just the shape Zeus assumes to rape Leda but also that bird on the waters at Coole Park. The crumbling ancient tower, while connected both with the gyres and with Greek civilization, is also the place where the Yeatses set up housekeeping.

Once again, though, the poem does much more than deal with symbols only; just as the large symbols are made homely and personal, so is the tragedy of war. The tone of the poem is set by the marvelous ambiguity of the final line of the first stanza: "All, all are in my thoughts to-night being dead." The intended meaning of the line appears to be that all the companions are dead, but the syntax is such that "being dead" also reflects on both "to-night" and "my thoughts." The rest of the poem contains all three partial meanings, as Yeats spends the evening "in death," reminiscing about his dead friends. Moreover, his thoughts are all of death; each time he begins to think on life his thoughts are wrenched back to death:

> I am accustomed to their lack of breath,
> But not that my dead friend's dear son,
> Our Sidney and our perfect man,
> Could share in that discourtesy of death.

> (CP, 131)

Later in the poem, he realizes that such discourtesy is the only end for "our Sidney":

Soldier, scholar, horseman, he,
As 'twere all life's epitome.
What made us dream that he could comb grey hair?

(CP, 133)

The speaker realizes here, in Stanza XI, that an uncommon man such as Gregory or Sidney can expect no common life or death: he died in what was seen as the glamorous death—if such a thing is possible—of World War I, the aviator's death in action. Though the poet catalogues Gregory's achievements in life, he is inevitably brought back to the fact of his death: "but a thought / Of that late death took all my heart for speech" (CP, 188). The war, unmentioned save for the epithet "soldier" and Gregory's rank in the title, is brought into the poem not as a general calamity but as a single, local (although noteworthy) loss. The tragedy of war is not lessened, nor does the comparison with Sidney, however much the reader sixty years later may feel it hyperbolic, affect that tragedy. The poem is ultimately concerned with human loss and waste of life; the rest is embellishment.

"An Irish Airman Foresees His Death" emphasizes the wanton waste of the war:

Those that I fight I do not hate,
Those that I guard I do not love;
My country is Kiltartan Cross,
My countrymen Kiltartan's poor,
No likely end could bring them loss
Or leave them happier than before.

(CP, 133)

The speaker's reasons for fighting have nothing to do with those espoused by the British propagandists: "Nor law, nor duty bade me fight, / Nor public men, nor cheering crowds . . ." Rather, he expresses that peculiar relation of Ireland to England during the war, that sense of being aligned with the enemy, of harboring no animosity toward the opponent.

Moreover, the feelings the speaker expresses, that he has no political or national interest in the war, present a knowledge that must have been widespread in Ireland: no direct link existed between the fighting on the continent and Irish independence. A British victory changed nothing, since Ireland remained a captive state, nor would a German conquest, in all probability, have affected matters—Yeats, like his speaker, is shrewd enough to see German assistance to Ireland for what it was, an act of war against England, not a blow for liberty. The Kaiser was no Lafayette. Such an attitude makes this poem characteristically Irish, a work of complex political and personal affiliations. The war offers the speaker no opportunity to advance or preserve any cause he believes in.

What it does offer him is the possibility of a heroic life and death:

> A lonely impulse of delight
> Drove to this tumult in the clouds;
> I balanced all, brought all to mind,
> The years to come seemed waste of breath,
> A waste of breath the years behind
> In balance with this life, this death.
>
> (CP, 133–134)

Yeatsian heroism in this poem, as in many others, closely resembles existentialism on several points, especially in its emphasis on solitary action and on courageous pursuit of doomed enterprises. It is the "lonely impulse of delight" that sends the speaker off to fight, and the tone of individuality is set by the triple emphasis of the first line's "*I* know that *I* shall meet *my* fate" [italics mine]. Similarly, the repetition of "waste of breath" at the end of line 14 and the beginning of line 15 in connection with the other possibilities life offers serves to emphasize the attractiveness of the airman's life and death. One can read this poem back into the preceding poem, as Yeats's attempt to justify what seems, from the perspective of Thoor Ballylee, a senseless death. Such a reading offers, whether one identifies the speaker as Gregory or not, an understanding of how any nonheroic life, no matter how successful or comfortable, fails in comparison with the heroic life, no matter how momentary.

The solitary man, too, takes on a sort of heroism by the mere fact of his solitude, by not being part of the rabble. There is nothing about the action of "The Fisherman" reminiscent of the Irish airman's death, and yet the poet holds him in the same sort of admiration:

> Maybe a twelvemonth since
> Suddenly I began,
> In scorn of this audience,
> Imagining a man,
> And his sun-freckled face,
> And grey Connemara cloth,
> Climbing up to a place
> Where stone is dark under froth,
> And the down-turn of his wrist
> When the flies drop in the stream;
> A man who does not exist,
> A man who is but a dream;
> And cried, "Before I am old
> I shall have written him one
> Poem maybe as cold
> And passionate as the dawn."

> (CP, 146)

The great majority of humanity, including Irishmen, hold no attraction for Yeats. He writes with distaste for the paudeen, beginning at least in *Responsibilities*, and his writings on Parnell demonstrate his feelings that Parnell was brought down as much by his "friends" as his enemies. Other people, and other people's beliefs and visions, are not to be trusted, hence the emphasis on the solitary man and the artist's loyalty to his own "journey towards beauty and truth." The imagined fisherman, the man dressed quietly who picks his own way among the rocks in the dawn, suits Yeats perfectly as a metaphor for the poetic act. Yeats, writing in his tower in the midst of turmoil and strife at home and abroad, finds in the lonely casting of flies at dawn (for he is no longer the poet of twilight) an apt symbol for the writing of his lyrics. He, like his fisherman, must pursue his own course, heedless of the rabble. The closing statement, with its hope of a special poem for a special audience, displays a major change from the Yeats of the Celtic Twilight. No longer does he feel the need to write of the common legends because he is writing for an Irish audience. Now a single, cold, hard, heroic poem will suffice, and this poem, whatever its successes or failures on other levels, achieves that hard, delicate tone he desires.

Of course, as Louis MacNeice points out, Yeats's conception of heroism is not limited to the artistic life:

> I do not mean that Yeats remained a disciple of Art for Art's sake; we have already seen how he deviated from that conception. Art for Art's sake defeated its own end because Art was thought of almost solely in terms of form, whereas the material of art is life and matter conditions form. . . . The paradox of poetry is like the paradox of individual freedom. An individual is not less free but more free, if he recognizes the factors which condition him and adjusts to his context; a poem is not less of a poem, but more of a poem, if it fulfills its business of corresponding to life.[9]

The events in Ireland during the war years make it impossible for Yeats to ignore them in his work. Although he can refuse a request for a war poem, "We have no gift to set a statesman right," he cannot maintain an aesthetic posture after 1916, even if he wants to (which is unlikely). While the death of Major Gregory in 1918 might be dismissed by some as an event of local interest, the circumstances of the Easter Rebellion are both major and public. Even so, Yeats is able to draw it into himself, to make the reader aware of the personal significance of this national event:

> I have met them at close of day
> Coming with vivid faces

From counter or desk among grey
Eighteenth-century houses.
I have passed with a nod of the head
Or polite meaningless words,
Or have lingered awhile and said
Polite meaningless words,
And thought before I had done
Of a mocking tale or a gibe
To please a companion
Around the fire at the club,
Being certain that they and I
But lived where motley is worn:
All changed, changed utterly:
A terrible beauty is born.

(CP, 177–178)

The tragic seriousness of the events that give rise to the poem
are contrasted in this first section with the casual pettiness of
the speaker's relations with the principals. Until the final two
lines, the emphasis rests entirely on the common insignifi-
cance of the interactions between the speaker and the rebels,
as the repetition of "polite meaningless words" suggests.
Then, too, there is an air of comfort, of middle-class-ism in
this section, with its "grey eighteenth-century houses" and
men around the fire at the club. The safety and insularity of
the middle class stand foremost in the poet's mind, and yet
they are gone. The tone of the section contrasts with the ease
of the actions: the phrasing of "polite meaningless words"
suggests the waste of those words, and the "Being certain
that they and I / But lived where motley is worn" carries with
it the implication of error. One rarely refers to one's past as-
suredness unless it is proved to be unfounded. In this case,
he is aware of the insufficiency of his understanding of the
rebels, not so much that he misjudged them but that their
participation in the rebellion and their subsequent deaths
and imprisonments have taken them out of the ordinary
realm of personal judgment. That single action turns back on

all others, forcing the speaker to reevaluate his attitudes toward them.

The second section examines further this shift in attitudes, pushing the meaninglessness of the first to greater specificity. The people appear, along with Yeats's earlier opinions of them; what the reader finds is not that the poet's relationships were inconsequential, but that they were invalidated by the rebellion and its outcome:

> He, too, has resigned his part
> In the casual comedy;
> He, too, has been changed in his turn,
> Transformed utterly:
> A terrible beauty is born.

> (CP, 178)

The "casual comedy" refers not to anything specific in the Yeats-MacBride acquaintance but to the whole sphere of ordinary existence that finds itself invalidated by these extraordinary events. MacBride's new "reality" has turned his earlier reality—and the poet's opinion of him—to a dream. Moreover, that which is transformed becomes more specific in this section: the conspirators, particularly those executed, have undergone the transformation. This additional detail adds a tension to the final line not found in its first appearance; the birth of the terrible beauty is inextricably linked to the deaths of sixteen men. The two most striking changes in this world, birth and death, are, in this poem, finally inseparable. Yeats contrasts this radical transformation with natural change in the third section, for this change is not moment by moment but rather permanent, frightening, apocalyptic. The beauty is terrible.

The poet's ambivalence toward the rebellion and its consequences runs through the final movement of the poem. The conspirators provide him with a nearly perfect example of heroism, and yet their actions may finally have been foolhardy:

Was it needless death after all?
For England may keep faith
For all that is done and said.
We know their dream; enough
To know they dreamed and are dead;
And what if excess of love
Bewildered them till they died?

(CP, 179)

Heroism is here coupled with lost alternatives; the executed rebels have become national monuments, icons (Yeats sometimes employs them as such in his later work), while at the same time they have cut short possibilities the poet sees as perhaps more satisfactory. Yeats does not condemn them, however. He employs an *and* rather than a *but* in the lines, "And what if excess of love / Bewildered them till they died," indicating not a change of heart on his part but a recognition that heroism and error are not mutually exclusive. So the poet finds himself confronted by laudable heroism coupled with dubious wisdom, neither of which can be overlooked. His ambivalence toward the situation appears in other poems as well, notably in "Sixteen Dead Men":

But who can talk of give and take
What should be and what not
While those dead men are loitering there
To stir the boiling pot?

(CP, 180)

The slain leaders of the rebellion, whatever they gave Ireland, have removed the possibility of rational, leisurely debate. Not only, as the poem suggests, can corpses not participate in discussion with the living, but the deaths have incited the living to a point where reason is no longer an option.

The situation offers no clear paths to resolution, and yet Yeats, as poet, must reach some resolution even if, as citizen, he cannot. To this end, he slips quite self-consciously into his role as poet:

> I write it out in a verse—
> MacDonagh and MacBride
> And Connolly and Pearse
> Now and in time to be,
> Wherever green is worn,
> Are changed, changed utterly:
> A terrible beauty is born.
>
> (CP, 179–180)

The poetic resolution incorporates the personal ambivalence, for he has to pass no judgment, to reach no decision about ultimate good or evil. At the same time, he does not retreat from the scene. His poetry is an instrument of understanding, something that allows him to take stock of the situation, rather than a political weapon that forces him to find an answer to it. It is enough to recognize the apocalyptic nature of the times.

That sense of apocalypse is taken up again in "The Second Coming," this time connected with the material of *A Vision*. The first line introduces the gyre in a way altogether more satisfactory and sensible than that of "Demon and Beast," which immediately precedes it: "Turning and turning in a widening gyre" makes a good deal more sense than "Now gyring down and perning there," especially to the reader not initiated into Yeats's visionary system. The image of the falcon sweeping out higher and farther until out of range of its master is marvelously vivid; it gives life and clarity to the otherwise abstract third line, "Things fall apart; the centre cannot hold." The falcon warrants the reader's attention for a second reason; although Yeats calls the final section of *A Vision* "Dove or Swan," he uses neither in this poem about the birth of a new age. Whether or not the falcon or a desert bird will be the instrument of the new annunciation, here they are certainly a harbinger of the new age as it moves out in a gyre that is inaccessible to its human master. The poem's visionary aspect, however, does not exist alone, and the next five lines bring it back to the familiar world:

> Mere anarchy is loosed upon the world,
> The blood-dimmed tide is loosed, and everywhere
> The ceremony of innocence is drowned;
> The best lack all conviction, while the worst
> Are full of passionate intensity.

(CP, 184–185)

At the time he writes this poem, in January 1919,[10] Yeats has just seen Europe come through the bloodiest five years in history, and the "blood-dimmed tide" must seem to him a very apt metaphor for the tremendous loss of life. Moreover, the political situation in his own country suggests to him that anarchy threatens to supplant order altogether. This also is a great period for Wobblies and anarchists of all descriptions, particularly in America, although it is unclear how much attention Yeats gives to those developments. The phrase, "Mere anarchy," is marvelous in its performance of two duties at once: while "mere" suggests that it is only anarchy, with nothing positive coming from it, there is also the trace of the older meaning of total or absolute, hinting that anarchy may completely overrun the world. These two destructive forces drown the "ceremony of innocence," that prewar "casual comedy" of "Easter 1916." The sense in Yeats's poetry at this time is very strong that the world of a few years earlier is lost irretrievably. The final two lines of the first section also recall "Easter 1916," for it is in that poem that we see Yeats unable to reach a resolution, "lacking all conviction," in contrast to someone like MacBride, certainly one of the worst in the poet's mind, who is "full of passionate intensity."

The poem then shifts in the second section into a vision of apocalypse. This Yeatsian version, true to his *Vision*, is not an absolute end but both an end and a beginning, although that lessens the terror not at all:

> The darkness drops again; but now I know
> That twenty centuries of stony sleep
> Were vexed to nightmare by a rocking cradle,
> And what rough beast, its hour come round at last,
> Slouches towards Bethlehem to be born?
>
> (CP, 185)

This birth of a god has very little to do with the standard, mild, Christian version of the birth of Christ, aside from the choice of Bethlehem, and the same tone appears in related poems, particularly "The Mother of God," "The terror of all terrors that I bore / The Heavens in my womb" (CP, 244). Terror is the word that colors the human in its interactions with the divine, and the poet's "terrible beauty" seems to have nearly universal applicability to his poems of the transition from one era to the next, which so often end on a questioning note:

> This love that makes my heart's blood stop
> Or strikes a sudden chill into my bones
> And bids my hair stand up?
>
> (CP, 244)

This terror is a major aspect introduced into Yeats's poetry in "The Second Coming," but it is not the only one. In fact, the poem may be even more significant for its integration of the mundane and the mythological. Since 1917, the two aspects both have appeared in the poetry but separately; "The Phases of the Moon" and "The Double Vision of Michael Robartes," for instance, concern themselves almost exclusively with the material from *A Vision*, whereas that material appears only as isolated references in the poems of more common reality. "The Second Coming," then, stands as one of the first successful attempts to fuse the two and, as such, marks a shift in the method of his later work. Although his new visionary schema may have developed in response to events of the times, his integration of the commonplace, the political, and the prophetic was an achievement by no means lightly won.

In his work of the late teens and early twenties, Yeats introduces his new poetic interests, the material of *A Vision* and the political realities of Ireland. With the poems from *The Tower* and the volumes that follow it, his work begins to take on something like Northrop Frye's "ideal order" on a smaller scale. In "The Wild Swans at Coole" and *Michael Robartes and the Dancer* the visionary and political elements fail to coalesce convincingly, for the most part; and such poems as "The Phases of the Moon" and "The Saint and the Hunchback" remain didactic exercises, lacking the engaging human qualities of his best verse. In his later work, he achieves a more suitable integration of these two new elements, owing largely to his ability to incorporate his visionary material, as well as the politics of Ireland, into his personal experience.

The gyres, for instance, appear only rarely in the later work as themselves, but the poet calls often upon their homelier cousins, the tower and the winding stair. These two appear quite frequently and usually together: just as one gyre is philosophically untenable without another for Yeats, so is the tower, in a very mundane way, useless without a winding stair. Moreover, the two images are usually local and as solid as Thoor Ballylee itself; they overcome the problem of abstraction inherent in the gyres. "Meditations in Time of Civil War" makes just such use of them:

> An ancient bridge, and a more ancient tower,
> A farmhouse that is sheltered by its wall,
> An acre of stony ground
> Where the symbolic rose can break in flower,
> Old ragged elms, old thorns innumerable,
> The sound of the rain or sound
> Of every wind that blows;

> The stilted water-hen
> Crossing stream again
> Scared by the splashing of a dozen cows;
>
> A winding-stair, a chamber arched with stone,
> A grey stone fireplace with an open hearth,
> A candle and a written page.
>
> (CP, 199)

The introduction of tower and stair here is casual, off-handed, and in keeping with the overall tone of the poem. This poem is in many ways central to his later work, introducing themes, symbols, phrases he will use time and again. Its greatest contribution, however, may well be its melding of personal, visionary, and political elements into a single unity. This is neither a war poem nor a private poem, and the reader must be careful to remember the whole title. The meditation is present, to be sure, as the speaker looks at himself, his neighborhood, his home, and his descendants, but it is a meditation springing from the civil strife around him. The clash of the brutality of the conflict and the casual, off-handed tone of the poem creates tremendous tension:

> We are closed in, the key is turned
> On our uncertainty, somewhere
> A man is killed, or a house burned,
> Yet no clear fact to be discerned:
> Come build in the empty house of the stare.
> A barricade of stone or of wood;
> Some fourteen days of civil war;
> Last night they trundled down the road
> That dead young soldier in his blood:
> Come build in the empty house of the stare.
>
> (CP, 202)

The civil war is an inescapable fact for the poet; he has been a close observer of the Irish political scene for years, and now, as Ellmann points out: "At Thoor Ballylee in 1922 the symbolical tower seemed likely to be attacked by unsymbolical men and weapons at any moment, and husband and wife frequently ran to the window to look out when the sounds of gunfire were especially close."[11] The "retreat," then, into the private world of his tower is an act less of escapism than of simple self-preservation: Yeats turns inward because he cannot go out. In section five, "The Road at My Door," not only is the road at his door but so are representatives of both warring factions. This situation forces him into his tower to look out at the stare's nest. Throughout the poem, he contrasts the quietness of the tower to the violence outside, and in the refrain, "Come build in the house of the stare," he juxtaposes the calm, homely plea for constructive actions with the destructive power of the war. Even the descriptions of the fighting are unhysterical, almost meditative: "somewhere / A man is killed, or a house burned, / Yet no clear fact to be discerned."

The potential for destruction nevertheless remains in the poem, and images of that destruction abound, particularly, as always, in the image of the tower:

> May this laborious stair and this stark tower
> Become a roofless ruin that the owl
> May build in the cracked masonry and cry
> Her desolation to the desolate sky.

> (CP, 201)

On first reading this passage seems to be a curse, but when the rest of the poem is read back against it, it appears more a warning than a curse. An actual peril presents itself to those who consort with fools or who, becoming too caught up in "business with the passing hour," lose their sense of perspective. Such people will need no curse; they will let an old, irrelevant tower fall into disrepair through their own lack of interest. The crumbling tower finds an analog in the empty stare's nest, and it is on the top of the tower, leaning upon a broken stone, that the poet sees "phantoms of hatred."

The destruction and tumult continues in "Nineteen Hundred and Nineteen":

> Many ingenious lovely things are gone
> That seemed sheer miracle to the multitude,
> Protected from the circle of the moon
> That pitches common things about.

> (CP, 204)

Seem is perhaps the key word in this poem, for the imagined reality of earlier days has been shattered by the harsh brutality of the Black and Tans. Here, in the first stanza, the poet realizes that those seemingly immutable "ingenious lovely things" are in fact under the moon's sway and therefore subject to change. The present reality changes everything:

> Now days are dragon-ridden, the nightmare
> Rides upon sleep: a drunken soldiery
> Can leave the mother, murdered at her door,
> To crawl in her own blood, and go scot-free;
> The night can sweat with terror as before
> We pieced our thoughts into philosophy,
> And planned to bring the world under a rule
> Who are but weasels fighting in a hole.

> (CP, 205)

This poem speaks back to, and is informed by, "Easter 1916," for in this poem Yeats shows much more vividly the ways in which his world is "changed utterly." There is a more general sense of terror in the later poem, for where only the conspirators in the Easter Rebellion were punished, no one is safe from the violence of the Royal Irish Constabulary. Everything must be redefined in terms of the present situation, and so those who, with the poet, would have changed the world are reduced to "weasels fighting in a hole." Men and monuments lose all value:

A man in his own secret meditation
Is lost amid the labyrinth that he has made
In art or politics;

                 *   *   *   *

. . . if our works could
But vanish with our breath
That were a lucky death,
For triumph can but mar our solitude.

(CP, 206)

Under the influence of the events of 1919 the poet finds himself confronted by the seemingly opposite situation from that
of the poem's opening. The spirit of negation becomes here
an active force, not merely levelling monuments but turning
them against their creators. Mockery, then, becomes spirit of
the age, counting among its victims mockers and mocked
alike. And yet, out of this demonic ne plus ultra, Yeats writes
his poem. Seemingly convinced that this poem, this monument, will turn back against him, mocking, he goes ahead
and writes it. Whether such persistence attests to his capacity
to believe or to doubt, it in any event demonstrates his desire
to peer over the sometimes ugly head of event into the chasm
of history.

Whatever the merits of Yeats's system may be for anyone
else, it allows him to view history as an ongoing process
rather than a discontinuous series of occurrences, so that
"Easter 1916" leads not to nihilism but to a second coming,
so that the tumult of the rebellions and the civil strife leads
not to the end but to an end, not to apocalypse but to another
Leda. Images of a new annunciation, either of Leda or Mary,
recur throughout his later poetry. In "Among School Children," the poet is obsessed with the notion of Leda as he sees
it embodied by, presumably, Maud Gonne. Yeats makes, in
this poem, one of his greatest attempts to bring together all
aspects of his thought and life, to achieve Unity, if not of
being, at least of poetics. His relationship with Maud Gonne,
his role in Irish politics, his advancing age, his mythology of

history and thought—all find a place in this poem, which in its final stanza looks forward to the ideal of Unity of Being:

> Labour is blossoming or dancing where
> Body is not bruised to pleasure soul,
> Nor beauty born out of its own despair,
> Nor blear-eyed wisdom out of midnight oil.
>
> (CP, 214)

He appears to long for this unity because he finds only fragmentation or incompleteness in his world, where a Ledean body holds only the promise, not the fulfillment of a new age, where old men are reduced to "Old clothes upon old sticks to scare a bird."

And yet the promise remains. The Ledean image is not always thwarted; it finds its most notable fulfillment in, of course, "Leda and the Swan," a poem made almost inevitable by "The Second Coming." The language of the two poems, the brutality and terror they express, makes them companion pieces, along with "The Mother of God," so that one is tempted to say, with MacNeice:

> Yeats's obsession during this period with the myth of Leda also signifies his belief that, in defiance of Aristotle, history has its roots in philosophy, that the eternal (Zeus) requires the temporal (Leda), further (for the myth is complex) that the human (Leda) requires the animal (the swan), that God and Nature in fact require each other and that the world will only make sense in terms of an incarnation.[12]

Unfortunately, MacNeice stops short of a full explanation of the myth, neglecting the terrifying aspects of those encounters. The "twenty centuries of stony sleep" are not awakened, but "vexed to nightmare," and it is a "terrible beauty" that is born in the Easter poem. The prospect of the new age is thoroughly terrifying; the curtain hiding it from the poet lifts only for a moment, long enough to reveal a frightening image, and then drops again. These poems of second comings share with

Eliot's "Journey of the Magi" a sense of mortal fright. Moreover, the annunciation itself partakes of the terror in the air:

> How can those terrified vague fingers push
> The feathered glory from her loosening thighs?
> And how can body, laid in that white rush,
> But feel the strange heart beating where it lies?
>
> (CP, 211–212)

The fright inspired in the human by the animal/divine is
closely akin to that of "The Mother of God," in which the
terror of the act itself is exceeded only by the terror inspired
by the knowledge that she bears "The Heavens in my womb."
In "Leda and the Swan," though, the fright is enhanced by
the physical brute presence of the swan and by the indifference of Zeus once he has raped her. Such indifference alters
significantly MacNeice's notion of how the eternal requires
the temporal. And, finally, the terror promises to continue:

> A shudder in the loins engenders there
> The broken wall, the burning roof and tower
> And Agamemnon dead.
>
> (CP, 212)

The chaos and violence of the end of a cycle ceases, only to
be replaced by war and treachery in the new cycle. In short,
Yeats finds small comfort in the promise of a new age, although he finds manifold terrors in the end of his own era.

Again in this poem Yeats employs familiar images to convey his visionary-poetic message. The swan has been turning
up regularly in his poetry for a long while, quite often as the
unmythologized white birds of Coole Park. Its use in this
poem stands as an attempt to make the mythology part of his
own poetic cosmos. The "broken wall, the burning roof and
tower" represent the same attempt, though on a more sweeping scale. Once again the poet finds that the crumbling battlements of Thoor Ballylee can serve his poetic purposes, for the
broken tower is the ideal emblem for the destruction of Troy

and hence for the historical cycle ushered in by the rape of Leda. Furthermore, the tower is a powerful symbol for Yeats because it is his own; through it he can make connections with his own life, with the Irish political situation (since the tower serves him so well in poems of the rebellions and the civil war), and with the scholarly or poetic life in general (a role it plays in many of the *Vision* poems). The tower, therefore, is an ideal symbol for performing several functions at once, an important capacity in such a compact poem. "Leda and the Swan," then, becomes the poet's own, part of his own mythology rather than someone else's and as much related to his era as to its own. His ability to absorb the material into his own poetic universe saves the poem from being a mere curiosity.

This ability to connect various elements into a private poetic universe marks a shift from his earlier verse, when his use of Irish elements, for instance, was largely along the lines of common typology, and it allows him, in his *Last Poems*, to bring everything he knows to bear on his poetry. Arra Garab has documented in *Beyond Byzantium* the totalizing impulse in the late poems:

> We see in his poetry of 1929–1939 such familiar Yeatsian motifs as the relation of body and soul, of life to art, of the artist to his past; the question of artifice versus actuality; the meaning of history, and the ends to which men and all creation move; the memory of "beautiful lofty things" both personal and public, poetic and political. Newer images emerge and soon come to crown the apocalyptic landscape formed by his heightened imagination.[13]

All past characters, past themes, past forms reappear in his final volume, although with a difference from their previous appearances: he employs them not as nostalgia, not merely as he had earlier, but as he needs them for the work at hand. Ballads are not simple imitations of older forms but instead become vehicles for tough, bitter, often ironic tales. Refrains are not so much logical outcomes as ironic counterpoints, as in "The O'Rahilly" with its *"How goes the weather."* Pearse,

Cuchulainn, Lady Gregory, and Plotinus, the gyres, and the Sidhe, all appear side by side in the *Last Poems* in a way that rarely occurs elsewhere in Yeats. Several possible reasons for this ecumenism suggest themselves.

The first is that the poet, knowing he is nearing the end of his life, looks back over that life and others that ran alongside it, judging their progress. From at least "Among School Children," Yeats has been concerned with the idea that old age is no satisfactory extension of the promise of youth, and in "Why Should Not Old Men Be Mad?" he makes his point more explicitly:

> Why should not old men be mad?
> Some have known a likely lad
> That had a sound fly-fisher's wrist
> Turn to a drunken journalist;
> A girl that knew all Dante once
> Live to bear children to a dunce;
> A Helen of social welfare dream,
> Climb on a wagonette to scream.
>
> (CP, 333)

Yeats sees the flowering of Ireland, and of his own talent, as something irrevocably lost, "a thing never known again." He has watched his hope of an Olympian Ireland, a place of intellect, vision, and liberty, disintegrate into murder, civil chaos, and paudeenism. He has watched his own gift become less easy to call up, his own physical self fall victim to the ravages of old age. And so his last work may stand as an attempt to bring the young poet and the old together, to reevaluate not only himself but his country and its recent history as well. Such a notion finds support in the numerous poems of Parnell, Pearse and Connolly, de Valera and others in the final volume.

Nor does his intermingling of previous work limit itself to the more overtly political poems such as "The Statues." In "News for the Delphic Oracle," for example, hardly a political poem, Yeats uses figures from both his early and later work:

Man-picker Niamh leant and sighed
By Oisin on the grass;
There sighed amid his choir of love
Tall Pythagoras.
Plotinus came and looked about,
The salt-flakes on his breast,
And having stretched and yawned awhile
Lay sighing like the rest.

(CP, 323)

The figures from the Celtic Twilight and those from the period of *A Vision* share the scene equally in this first section,
whereas in most of the earlier poetry they are an either-or
proposition. Moreover, they are equally the targets of his
irony, his reference to them as "the golden codgers," an irony
that ultimately must be seen as self-irony, since those figures
are products of the poet's earlier work. The following stanza
exhumes yet another previous image, the dolphins bearing
spirits on their backs, this one picked up from "Byzantium."
This image, too, fails to fully satisfy his needs, for it is, as are
Niamh and Plotinus, overly spiritual; the dolphins are mire
and blood but the Innocents are not. And so, in the final
movement, the poet introduces sensual presences into the
version of paradise he offers to the Oracle.[14]

A similar, and surely the most famous, use of bygone images in the interest of self-irony occurs in "The Circus Animals' Desertion":

Maybe at last, being but a broken man,
I must be satisfied with my heart, although
Winter and summer till old age began
My circus animals were all on show,
Those stilted boys, that burnished chariot,
Lion and woman and the Lord knows what.

(CP, 335)

The poem takes on in this first stanza a self-mocking tone,
aimed not only at the poet in his old age and despair but at

his younger, creative self as well. To call his images "circus animals," with all the attendant associations of hoop jumping and tricks by rote, immediately focuses the reader's attention on the sham quality of poetry, the sideshow artifice of symbolism. In the enumeration of old themes, he pauses at the end of each stanza to remind the reader that he, the ringmaster, has been duped by his own artifice:

Players and the painted stage took all my love,
And not those things that they were emblems of.

(CP, 336)

With this statement Yeats joins any number of his critics who charge him with lacking humanity, with choosing artifice over the world.[15] Of course, such a ploy works to distract our attention from the profoundly human quality of his poetry—the vacillation, the struggle to come to terms with nation, history, and fellow man, the continual exploration of his own heart.

He surely is aware that he misrepresents himself, and the final stanza points to a reason:

Those masterful images because complete
Grew in pure mind, but out of what began?
A mound of refuse or the sweepings of a street,
Old kettles, old bottles, and a broken can,
Old iron, old bones, old rags, that raving slut
Who keeps the till. Now that my ladder's gone,
I must lie down where all the ladders start
In the foul rag-and-bone shop of the heart.

(CP, 336)

That the images are masterful and complete suggests that they, not he, have outlived their poetic usefulness; when they become purely intellectual, and thereby dissociated from the human heart, they can no longer serve as poetic images, for poetry is concerned, ultimately, with humanity and life. And so the poet has been searching among them for his theme in vain: theirs is a world of pure artifice, no country for old poets. Rather, he must look into himself once again, must lie down "in the foul rag-and-bone shop of the heart," because, however much he represents its unappealing aspects, his heart is the only fertile ground for poetry. Whether or not the poem is intended as a clearing out of what has gone before falls into the realm of pure speculation, but the movement of the work suggests a renewed dedication of his poetry to humanity. This rededication is echoed in "Under Ben Bulben":

> Poet and sculptor, do the work,
> Nor let the modish painter shirk
> What his great forefathers did,
> Bring the soul of man to God.
> Make him fill the cradles right.

(CP, 342)

There is no difference, finally, between proper craftsmanship and the study of humanity: to fail in one is to shirk the other. While the poet is concerned here with "singing the people," his attitude casts light back on his earlier sentiments that bad poetry in the cause of nationalism performs a disservice to the nation.

Moreover, this last poem brings to our attention something we have known all along: when he says humanity, he really means the Irish. Whatever direction his poetry has taken him, it has always brought him back again. He moves, not from Irish poets to poets in general in this poem, but vice versa. And so he returns, after all his exotic spiritual and intellectual ramblings, to Drumcliff churchyard and the horsemen of faerie, with an epitaph that misleadingly points toward disaffection with humanity, while actually reminding us that individual life and death merely punctuate the larger cycle of humanity:

> Under bare Ben Bulben's head
> In Drumcliff churchyard Yeats is laid.
> An ancestor was rector there

Long years ago, a church stands near,
By the road an ancient cross.
No marble, no conventional phrase;
On limestone quarried near the spot
By his command these words are cut:
Cast a cold eye
On life, on death
Horseman, pass by!

(CP, 344)

6 / So Much Depends

Disjunctive Poetics
and the Poem
Sequence

Early on in Virginia Woolf's *Mrs. Dalloway*, a skywriter plies his trade over London, witnessed by residents throughout the city: at Buckingham Palace, in Regent's Park, on the Mall, at Clarissa Dalloway's house in Westminster. Aside from the new technology itself, there is nothing remarkable in this picture. What is noteworthy, however, is the characteristically Modernist viewpoint and narrative stance Woolf employs in the scene. While the airplane provides a physical or psychological center for the movements of diverse people, she neither shows it objectively nor uses it as a platform from which to view and thereby unify the city below. Rather, we see the plane through the characters' eyes and thoughts, so that it becomes the focal point for a host of sensory impressions and visceral responses:

> So, thought Septimus, looking up, they are signalling to me. Not indeed in actual words; that is, he could not read the language yet; but it was plain enough, this beauty, this exquisite beauty, and tears filled his eyes as he looked at the smoke words languishing and melting in the sky and bestowing upon him in their inexhaustible charity and laughing goodness one shape after another of unimaginable beauty and signalling their intention to provide him, for nothing, for ever,

for looking merely, with beauty, more beauty! Tears ran down
his cheeks.[1]

While the response of Septimus Warren Smith, a shell-
shocked veteran who will commit suicide later in the day, is
more charged than most of his fellow citizens, it is nevertheless typical of their relationships to this bit of external reality.
He does not describe the plane directly, does not think of it
in any kind of objective sense. Instead, the plane is the stim-
ulus for his thoughts, so much so in his case that he barely
sees it (he appears to recognize only the letters) for what it is.

What Woolf gives the reader, then, is a new poetics, based
to a large extent on the young, exciting field of psychology.
Accepting the notion from various sources—William James,
Freud, Jung—that the real action of the mind lies below the
surface, the modern writer turns away from the level of overt
action and rhetoric as the focal point of art, away from the
level with which most earlier art had concerned itself.

If one agrees with James's notion of a stream of consciousness, then external events and objects become interesting not
so much for themselves as for the effects, the ripples they
cause in the stream. *Mrs. Dalloway*'s skywriter provides no
insight for the reader in and of himself, but he is the occasion
for manifold insights into characters and relationships. Lu-
crezia Warren Smith, for instance, points out the airplane
precisely because it is external, in the hope of drawing her
husband out of himself; Septimus, however, is so completely
lost to the outside world that he manages to internalize this
highly public form of communication: "they are signalling
to me."

Time and again, Modernist literature demonstrates a belief
by its makers in the primacy of individual consciousness as
the constitutive element of art. What really matters is not
"objective" reality (if indeed such a thing exists) but subjec-
tive perception. What we see, so far as we are concerned at
least, *is* reality, Stephen Dedalus' "ineluctable modality of the
visible." The major implication of such a belief for modern
poetics is its emphasis on the moment of awareness, on
epiphany and image, those precise instants when the outside

world causes ripples in the stream of consciousness. In turn, this faith in moments, in images, has led to a poetics of disjuncture and to a new kind of long poem as the dominant form in English. It is perhaps not too much to say that almost the whole of modern poetic practice depends on William Carlos Williams' little poem about a red wheelbarrow.

The early years of the century produced three separate groups of poetic innovators: the Georgian poets, the Sitwell group, and the Imagists. Although all three failed as sustained movements, each contributed elements to the larger field of modern poetry. The first two groups were decidedly minor, producing little work that has continued to be held in high esteem by the critical or poetic communities. The Georgians are often dismissed as the old guard, what the true modernists struggled to overthrow, yet such an easy dismissal overlooks the radical nature of the movement. As Geoffrey Bullough points out, Georgian poetry, while a throwback to Romanticism, represented a break with Imperial poetry of the same period, and the established poets of the day looked upon it with some horror.[2] Moreover, while the movement itself died down, some of its work in loosening the reins on traditional verse forms has survived, as one can see in the repeated comparisons of Philip Larkin's work to the Georgian poetry of Edward Thomas. The conversational diction and simplicity of their poetry, as Bullough further notes, has become something of a standard feature of some strains of modern poetry. Similarly, the work of the group gathered around the Sitwells ultimately came to little, yet much in that poetry foreshadows developments in other, more prominent poets. The spiritual despair, the often-forced gaiety, the combination of wit and bleakness of Sitwellian poetry shows up in many other writers' work in the century. Their work is, for the most part, ignored or forgotten because they had very little to say; their poetry had much surface but lacked substance.[3]

Of the three, Imagism is by far the most important school for modern verse at large, but even that significance is in spite of the movement's aims and practices. The goal of the movement, as the name implies, was to bring to poetry a new emphasis on the image as a structural, not ornamental, element. Growing out of French Symbolism and taking techniques, styles, and forms from Japanese haiku, tanka, and hokku, Chinese ideograms, classical Greek, and Provençal troubadour lyrics, Imagism reflects the diverse interests of its founders and their rather dilettantish nature.

While they included a number of very fine practitioners, among them F. S. Flint, D. H. Lawrence, Richard Aldington, T. E. Hulme, HD, William Carlos Williams, Carl Sandburg, and Amy Lowell, Ezra Pound remains for us the major spokesman and publicist for the group, as well as its preeminent practitioner. Pound, along with Aldington and HD, formulated, or at least put forward as having formulated, the three cardinal rules of the movement in "A Retrospect": direct treatment of the thing discussed; absolute economy of diction; and composition "in the sequence of the musical phrase, not in the sequence of the metronome."[4] At various times, others in the group expanded upon or modified those three initial rules, yet they stand as the basis for Imagist technique. In fact, the rules are descriptive rather than prescriptive; the group had been meeting in one form or another for a couple of years when Pound claimed to have formulated these precepts. Much of the philosophical basis for the school comes from Hulme's study of Henri Bergson's thought. Under Hulme's influence, the varied interests of the members jelled into a more or less cohesive body of theory, at least for a short time.[5]

The poetry produced by the group, although by no means uniform, shared certain characteristics. First of all, it was an attempt to put the creation of images at the center of the poetic act. The image is a sudden moment of truth, or as Pound describes it, "an intellectual and emotional complex in an instant of time."[6] It shares a good deal with other modern moments of revelation, from Gerard Manley Hopkins' "inscape" to James Joyce's "epiphany." The brevity of the Imagist poem, another characteristic, particularly of those produced early in the group's history, is a logical extension of the emphasis on the image. As an attempt to eschew rhetorical and narrative forms and to replace them with the "pure" poetic moment, the Imagist poem, existing almost solely for the creation of its image, completes its entire mission with the completion of that image.

Pound's "In a Station of the Metro" stands as the most famous, if not the most representative, of the poems produced by the Imagists:

> The apparition of these faces in the crowd;
> Petals on a wet, black bough.[7]

In its perfection, conciseness, and absolute reliance on a metaphorical leap, this poem far outstrips virtually all others in upholding the principles of "A Retrospect." Its success rests entirely on the reader's ability to buy into the particular vision of the poet. Pound offers no explanation, no excuse, no language of comparison. Interestingly, a great many Imagist poems hedge their bets by using simile rather than metaphor, and in the weakest of them the word "like" becomes obtrusive in its frequency. Not so with Pound. His faith in the accuracy of his perception, perhaps his confidence in the psychology of perception more generally, is so strong he simply throws out the image: the reader either gets it or does not. And having given the image to the reader, the poet's job is completed, the poem finished. The same can be said of the finest Imagist poems, as, for example, HD's "Oread"; either one sees the validity of her comparison of a vast forest of firs with the sea, or else the poem is a failure, utterly baffling.[8] The purity, the cleanness of presentation, puts a tremendous burden on the poet's ability to see or select an appropriate image, something that will work without explication for the reader.

A long poem of the type would simply be a series of discrete images whose relation to one another could only be inferred, since explicative transitions would be a violation of precept. The greater length of the poems produced under the leadership of Lowell (after Pound had renounced the movement in a fit of pique) evidences a loosening of form, a laxity of craftsmanship. The late poems are not so much transitional, pointing toward some new development, as they are decadent, indicative of the movement's demise.

That Imagism would be short-lived was almost inevitable. The goals and techniques of the movement were antithetical to sustaining even a poem of any duration, let alone a school. The tiny Imagist verse is much too confining to allow its creator much variety from one poem to the next. The chance to explore themes, ideas, beliefs simply does not exist, since that sort of argument-oriented poetry is what Imagism sought to replace. Yet even the proponents of Imagism had bigger plans than their espoused methods would allow. Pound, for instance, even while he was most closely associated with the group, was working on the plan for the *Cantos*. Nonetheless, even if Imagism lacked the qualities to make it a sustained movement, its methods have been adopted into a great majority of poems written in this century. Of course, Imagist techniques appear in Williams' *Paterson* or the *Cantos*, but they also show up in the work of non-Imagists, such as Allen Tate, T. S. Eliot, Sylvia Plath, Dylan Thomas, and make possible such later developments as surrealism and the "deep image" poetry of James Wright and Robert Bly.

Imagism, itself the product of diverse influences, is only one of a great many influences on modern poetry. Perhaps the single most important influence has been French Symbolism. The French have been instrumental in helping English and American literary communities recognize important but overlooked elements within their own ranks on numerous occasions over the last two centuries, but rarely has the contribution been greater than that of the Symbolists. The source of much Symbolist theory is Poe, whose work was largely ignored by Anglo-American critics. The French, however, saw in his darkly Romantic speculations, in the bleakness and horror of his work, even in his impulse toward dissipation, the vehicle appropriate to poetry on the modern predicament. In his own country, he may have been a gothic oddity; in France, he was a prophet. The work produced by his French followers—Jules Laforgue, Tristan Corbiere, Stephane Mallarmé, Charles Baudelaire, Arthur Rimbaud, and

Paul Verlaine—incorporated much from Poe: the darkness, the exploration of life's underside, the penchant for urban landscape, and most important, the centrality of the symbol.

Certainly symbols have always been used in poetry, and little that the Symbolists accomplished with symbols was entirely new. What was fresh and unique, however, was their insistence on the symbol as the structural raison d'être of the poem. No longer relegated to the status of ornament or occasional item, the symbol became for these men the goal one actively sought to achieve in the poem. Like so many of their modern followers, they were reacting against the Scylla and Charybdis of loose, discursive verse on the one hand and didactic, allegorical verse on the other. Also, like their followers, they mistrusted language, having seen too much bad poetry turned out by employing conventional "poetic" language. They therefore felt that the achievement of poetry must lie elsewhere than in the play of words. Their solution was to place heavy emphasis on the poetic moment, the symbol. The words can be copied by hollow imitation, but an empty symbol immediately reveals itself. They attempted to separate the symbolic radically from the allegorical use of imagery, and there is about much Symbolist poetry a vagueness that refuses to let the symbol be quite pinned down. In some of the followers of Symbolism, particularly in the work of the English poets of the 1890s, that vagueness drifts off into airy realms too thin for habitation.

Symbolism found its way into Anglo-American modern poetry by so many routes that it is nearly impossible to chronicle them all. Nevertheless, a few of the points of entry require mention. The earliest important mention of Symbolism is in Arthur Symons' famous book of 1899, *The Symbolist Movement in Literature.* Symons, along with Yeats and other poets of the Rhymers' Club, introduced the work of these Frenchmen to English audiences not only through essays and defenses but through original English poetry on Symbolist models. Giving as much attention to prose writers as to poets, Symons hails the new literary wind blowing from Paris as one that does not shrink from neurosis, nightmare, decadence, and that therefore is the appropriate literature for its society. Of Mallarmé he says, "All his life he has been haunted by the desire to create, not so much something new in literature, as a literature which should be itself a new art."[9] This sense of newness, of shocking, appalling novelty, was immediately grasped by defenders and vilifiers alike, and Symbolism itself became a symbol. Oscar Wilde could not have set the character of Dorian Gray so well in ten pages of description, at least for his immediate audience, as he does by having Dorian, at several key points in the novel, reading J. K. Huysmans' *A Rebours*. This first wave of enthusiasm, however, was mainly a matter of imitation; and if it largely died out before producing any major works of interest, it was because the writers who experimented in the mode were playing with an exotic toy, not working with an instrument fitted to their own machinery. Still, among the Rhymers, Yeats learned the lessons of Symbolism well enough to incorporate them into his own poetic style and vision throughout the rest of his career.

The second major attempt at importation, this one aiming for domestication, grew eventually into Imagism. If the work of Symons and Yeats was important because it showed such a thing as Symbolism existed, Imagism's importance lay in the translation of one movement from one century and one place into another in another century and another place. Imagism sought to further refine the terms of the symbol, so that emphasis fell first of all on the part that actually appears in the poem, the image. Pound, writing of the aims of Imagism, said that the symbolic function was one of the possible uses of the image, but that it should never be so primary that the poem is lost on a person for whom "a hawk is simply a hawk."

The third major importer of Symbolism into English is T. S. Eliot. He writes extensively about the Symbolists; he copies their style, even to the point of writing in French in some early poems; he openly acknowledges his debt in direct borrowings from their work; and, most importantly, he has produced the most complete example of a Symbolist poem in English, *The Waste Land*. In the use of urban landscape, the feverish, nightmarish quality of the imagery, the darkness of the vision, the layering of symbols and images within symbols and images, the citations of Laforgue and Baudelaire, *The Waste Land* demonstrates its creator's overwhelming debt to the Symbolists. The poem's centrality in the modern canon lends further weight to the significance of Symbolism for modern Anglo-American poetry. Knowingly or not, every poet who has found himself affected by Eliot's great work has also been affected by Baudelaire and company.

Symbolism is not, however, the only major influence on modern poetry. Another example of Eliot's importance as an arbiter of poetic taste and style is the resurrection of the English Metaphysical poets as models for modern verse. Long ignored by English critics, the Metaphysicals—John Donne, in particular—show the modern poet another use of a controlling metaphor. If the Symbolists reintroduced the poet to the symbol, Donne and his contemporaries—Andrew Marvell, George Herbert, Henry Vaughan, Richard Crashaw—showed him how to use it in extended forms. The conceit of the Metaphysical poem, like the symbol of the Symbolist poem, is an example of figurative language used not as ornament but as structural principle. The influence is positively antidotal; since the conceit of a Donne poem is used as a way of integrating metaphor with argument, the model served to overcome the limiting element of Imagism and, to a lesser extent, of Symbolism itself. Both the latter movements, since they eschewed argument as a poetic method, shut themselves off from the possibility of a sustained use. The Metaphysical conceit (and what is the image of the wasteland if not a conceit, a unifying metaphor?) allows Eliot to adapt these modern techniques, limited to very short uses in their own contexts, to a much longer, more elaborate structure.

Another, very different model for long poems comes from Walt Whitman, at least for American poets. Although the general opinion of Whitman is lower among writers from the early part of the century, in large measure due to his Romanticism, than among their later counterparts, he nonetheless exerts influence on poetry throughout the century. Whitman's great contribution is in the area of open form. The sometimes chatty, sometimes oratorical, usually freewheeling style of his poetry has done more to show the path away from iambic verse than any other single source. His influence is clear on poets such as Williams, Lawrence, Ginsberg and his fellow Beat poets, Charles Olson and the Black Mountain poets, yet he also often moves through less obvious channels, and virtually any poet who has experimented with open forms owes him a debt. Even a poet as strongly opposed in principle to the looseness of his verse as Pound finds he must accord Whitman grudging respect.[10] Indeed, it is that very openness, that looseness, that makes possible the long poem after Imagism. Whitman demonstrates to the American poet that long verse need not rely on prosodic regularity to maintain its pace, that it may proceed by the strength of its ideas, by its own rhythms rather than, as Pound puts it, "the sequence of the metronome," by the sheer power of the poet's voice and personality. The combination, then, of the ideals of Imagism and the example of Whitman points the way toward the long poems, the poem sequences, that have dominated so much of the field of extended verse in this century.

A further impetus toward long-form poetry is the distinctive interest in myth and archetype among modern writers. To be sure, all poetry is concerned with myth at some level, yet the modern involvement differs from anything before in that it is constantly aware that life is a series of rituals, often acted out unawares, by which humanity expresses its relation to the universal. The trend of literature from the Romantics to the Symbolists to the Modernists is toward a more and more symbolic understanding. At the same time, most of the great advances in thought in the last two centuries also have been along those same lines, reinforcing and at times leading literature further along toward the mythic. What makes Marxist thought possible, for example, is an understanding that the events in a single place are not isolated phenomena but rather elements in a pattern of class struggle that border on the ritual. The bourgeoisie in any society will eventually reach the point at which it rises up and overthrows feudal society, and will itself eventually be overthrown by the proletariat. More overtly mythic works that influence the modern artist are Sir James Frazer's *The Golden Bough* and Jessie

Weston's *From Ritual to Romance*, both of which demonstrate not the individual instance of ritual but the common pattern as the aspect worthy of comment. The work of Freud and Jung at the beginning of the century further added to the modern writer's interest in myth, for the works of both psychoanalysts point toward something new. Whereas Frazer and Weston examine mythic patterns as cultural phenomena, Freud and Jung demonstrate the ways in which individuals internalize them. Myth and archetype gain their power, then, not from the emphasis society places on them but through their unshakable hold on the individual consciousness.

The result of this thinking was a tremendous explosion of genuinely new literature, of poetry and fiction in which the quotidian acts of petty individuals take on meaning beyond their understanding because of the connection to the universal. Among the fruits of this new flowering, the *anni mirabiles* of 1922–1925, were the two most important works produced in English in this century, both too big for subsequent writers to ignore and too awesome to copy: *Ulysses* and *The Waste Land*. In his essay, "*Ulysses*, Order, and Myth," Eliot announces that in place of the traditional narrative method, the modern artist could henceforth use the mythic method, that fiction and poetry would gain power not from their isolated stories but through the connection of the stories to a universal pattern. Such a belief merely extends his thinking in "Tradition and the Individual Talent" that literature grows out of other literature, carrying it back to its earliest point, its origin, mythology. *The Waste Land* should have surprised no one familiar with Eliot's thinking; it fits perfectly with the ideas outlined in his essays.

This interest in myth, particularly myth as a totalizing and organizing structure, as a means to providing a comprehensive picture of the social or artistic problem at hand in any given work, has as its political corollary a tendency of the modern artist to become engaged in overarching, even totalitarian movements of both the left and the right. Here, one has only to think the disastrous involvement of that arch-Modernist, Ezra Pound, with Mussolini's fascism. Yet his plunge into the unreason of totalitarianism is merely the most spectacular example of widespread flirtation with political extremism practiced by so many modern writers: Dos Passos, Lawrence, Wyndham Lewis, Yeats, and even Eliot being among the most notable. Such seeking after answers in radical movements should not surprise us entirely; the political center, particularly to those who had experienced World War I, seemed to offer so few answers for stability or peace, so little structure, so little social justice, so little cohesiveness for the fragmented, often chaotic modern world, that communism and fascism, which both offer a mythos of order, would appeal, at least in their theoretical aspects. It should be said that, to their credit, most of those writers renounced the movements once they saw them in action, saw the betrayal of apparently high-minded idealism once it reached the realm of practical application.

In the literary field, this interest in totalizing structures of myth led to longer works of poetry as well as to fiction that broke away from established norms of narrative. Although *Ulysses* and *Finnegans Wake* are the most well-known, even notorious, examples of the new fiction, others abound: *Absalom, Absalom!*, perhaps even the whole of Faulkner's Yoknapatawpha novels; Lawrence's *The Plumed Serpent*; Dos Passos' *U.S.A.* all raise fiction to a mythic level. *U.S.A.* provides an especially interesting study in the context of the poem sequence. For one thing, it creates its own mythology of America, replete with important actions and moments captured in the "Camera Eye" and "Newsreel" sections and a pantheon of heroes and villains in the biographies—all laced through the fictional narrative. One has only to read the biographies of "Fighting Bob" La Follette or Eugene Debs to see the heightened language with which Dos Passos elevates characters to the plateau of romance. The novel is further interesting in that it stands closer to the poem sequence in form than perhaps any other novel. In its self-contained elements standing in unexplained and uncompromising juxtaposition, its sudden leaps, its mix of private, public, fictional, factual, and mythological elements, *U.S.A.* shares a great many devices with the modern sequence. It also shares a debt to Imagism. Linda W. Wagner has articulated five points that modern fictionists have drawn from Imagism, and of course, they also apply to that other extended form, the poem sequence:

> (1) the centrality of the image, the concrete representation as opposed to abstraction. (2) The objectivity of the presentation. . . .
> (3) Juxtaposition as a means of connecting single images, the placing of image against image with no literal transition so that the reader's apprehension of meaning depends on his immediate response to the montage of concrete detail. (4) Organ base, Pound's notion that every piece of writing must have a controlling tone and shape appropriate to its basic meaning. (5) Simplicity, rooted in directness and in the lack of poetic diction and theme, a nonallusive and uncomplicated style.[11]

It is perhaps the notion of radical juxtaposition that frees the modern artist more than any of the other four and indeed is a logical and necessary outgrowth of an insistence on the image as the main element of a poem. Twentieth-century writers would understand, from Freud, from Jung, from James, that the mind works in these sudden, violent leaps, and as Wagner's use of "montage" suggests, they would understand it from other art forms as well, including the new form of cinema. There may be nothing so liberating to established art as a new technology that provides new techniques and implications, and both poetry and prose narrative drew from film very early on, as Dos Passos' use of both "Newsreel" and "Camera Eye" techniques demonstrates. Ultimately, then, the disjuncture introduced into English and American poetry by the cult of the image demanded new forms of longer works, including the abandonment of the traditional long poem in favor of the poem sequence.

Several impulses come together more or less at once to create the poetics of disjuncture of modern verse. One, as we have discussed, is the inheritance of Imagism, the concentration on the intensely poetic moment almost to the exclusion of all else. Another is the sense of fragmentation in society and in consciousness that many modern writers express; although organic form is full of hazards, fragmented consciousness may in some cases require fragmentation in its treatment. More important are the general ambivalence and the distrust of language. The ambivalence of modern writers toward the world leads them also to suspect received forms, particularly those forms that suggest continuity and wholeness. Such completeness contradicts their experience of the world, in which things are fragmented, discontinuous, chaotic, intractable. To blithely write long, flowing poems in the manner of Tennyson would be to violate one's own experience of the world and one's own consciousness. Other literary forms come under suspicion as well, but the modern poet is particularly wary of sustained, regular verse. Even such artists as Philip Larkin or Yeats, who work in received forms, often take great pains to change them, to make them less regular. The corollary suspicion, this one received from the Symbolists, is of language itself. Language for the modern writer is a debased medium, loaded with connotations from previous usage, and the language of poetry can also be the language of propaganda and politics. The very medium, then, is hazardous. As Stan Smith notes, both the "raw material" of literature and the means of dealing with it involve "that highly organised phenomenon, language,"[12] and the writer is well aware of the ironies implicit in such an overlap.

These several forces come together to move the modern poem away from sustained forms and toward disjuncture and discontinuity, toward poetry that follows Poe's famous statements regarding long poems with a self-awareness Poe never demonstrated in his own verse. Again, in this as in so much else, *The Waste Land* is a principal work. The poem leaps from image to image, violently throwing together unconnected and even antithetical elements to produce a work that, although it draws heavily on earlier literature, is like nothing that has gone before. The links between the five main sections of the poem have particularly troubled readers, since they are not related in any immediately identifiable manner. Still, they do cohere, they do move toward some final point as a group that none of them achieves alone. Their cohesiveness is a function of each section's relation to the whole, rather than, as one might expect, the relations between successive sections.

When the disjunctive poetics of modern verse encounter the poet's desire to create works of large scale, as in *The Waste Land,* traditional forms necessarily must be scrapped. In very short lyrics, of course, there is no problem with the connection between sections, but in longer works, the sections must stand together in some logical fashion or risk the outrage heaped on Eliot's work when it first appeared. Even so, a poem can go on piling image upon image without respite for just so long before it breaks down, before the reader becomes irretrievably lost in the morass. To circumvent the problems raised by continuity in a disjunctive poetry, the modern writer turns to the poem sequence. The sequence has been defined variously, but the most satisfactory definition is a series of poems that are capable of standing alone but that take on greater significance through their mutual interaction, or as M. L. Rosenthal and Sally M. Gall describe it,

> a grouping of mainly lyrical poems and passages, rarely uniform in pattern, which tend to interact as an organic whole. It usually includes narrative and dramatic elements, and ratiocinative ones as well, but its structure is finally lyrical. Intimate, fragmented, self-analytical, open, emotionally volatile, the sequence meets the needs of the modern sensibility even when the poet aspires to tragic or epic scope.[13]

That is to say, the sequence is a long poem made of shorter poems. The sequence is a distinctively modern phenomenon and has its opposite number in what Joanne V. Creighton, in her study *Faulkner's Craft of Revision,* calls the "short-story composite." The composite is a book made up of chapters that are themselves stories; the stories can be read separately, as in an ordinary collection, but they also form a unified whole when read together. She cites Hemingway's *In Our Time* and Faulkner's *Go Down, Moses* as such works, in which the writer has given as much planning and work to the larger book's structure (as in a novel) as he has to the individual parts (as in a normal short-story collection).

The poem sequence is not the exclusive property of the twentieth century, of course. Many earlier examples can be cited, depending on how one judges such matters: Rimbaud's *A Season in Hell;* Whitman's *Leaves of Grass;* Rossetti's sonnet sequence, *The House of Life;* Morris' *The Earthly Paradise;* perhaps even going back to Shakespeare's sonnets and the *Divine Comedy.* Yet, in almost every case, the premodern sequence attempts to justify its disunity by displaying a unity between its sections, by talking its way through or over the gaps. By contrast, the modern sequence often works by silence, by exploiting the interstices, allowing ambiguity or multiple meanings to slip in through the cracks. The unexplained juxtaposition of elements adds to the possible meanings the work puts forth, because potential meanings remain potential, the poet ruling in favor of no one over all others.

In the loosest possible sense, any book of poems is a sequence, and the difference between any collection and, say, *Paterson* is simply one of intent and degree. So, in the twentieth century, sequences come in all denominations. Both Lawrence and Yeats experiment with sequencing fairly informally in their work. Lawrence often collects his poems around a theme or a subject or a method of creation and strings poems together by resonant phrasings, as in the group of poems whose central piece is "The Ship of Death." Yeats, too, carefully arranges poems in his books and, in his revisions, changes not only poems but the order of poems as well. He carefully works themes across poems in his books and sometimes even from one book to another, so aware is he of his poetry as a whole corpus, and often a single poem, as we have seen, can give a mistaken impression of the entirety of his thought, as in the case of the Byzantium poems. Because he is such a meticulous poet, careful always about his material and his treatments, sensitive to the echoes of his earlier work, and because he, like Lawrence, works within the framework of a coherent personal mythology, Yeats's poetry always gives a sense of planning, of sequencing. At the other end of the scale stands *The Waste Land,* which is not, strictly speaking, a sequence at all, yet which shares many characteristics: fragmentation, separate titles for its sections, certainly even length and scope. On this matter I stand at odds with Rosenthal and Gall, whose understanding of the genre is rather broader and who include the poem as a sequence, indeed as the foremost example of its kind in many ways. As this study makes abundantly clear, I am also willing to insist on its centrality in the Modernist canon, as well as its importance in helping us understand poem sequences. Still, it fails to meet one of the criteria: its separate sections cannot stand alone as poems. One cannot dissect the poem without making hash of it: its structure is too tight. The "Unreal city" refrain of "The Burial of the Dead" is picked up later in "The Fire Sermon," adding to the weight and meaning of each usage, the poem speaking back and forth to itself. Similarly, the use of Phlebas in "Death by Water" depends for its success to a great extent on the appearance of Mr. Eugenides in the previous section and the tarot card of the "drowned Phoenician sailor" of the first. The interdependence of the sections of the poem is so great that although it looks like a sequence, it is not. It is a long, fragmentary, disjointed, truly modern poem. To find a real poem sequence in Eliot, one must look to the end, to *Four Quartets.*

The Waste Land received the discontinuity that is so striking in it, and the feeling we associate with sequences, in large measure from the blue pencil of Ezra Pound. Pound's editorial assistance, as in the case of *In Our Time,* nearly always took the form of radical deletion, and in this poem he cut much transitional and explanatory material, with the result of a formal jumpiness that reinforces the cultural and personal neurasthenia. One must look, though, to Pound's own work to find an early important example of a poem sequence.

Both *Homage to Sextus Propertius* and *Hugh Selwyn Mauberley* are early sequences by Pound and, while not mere exercises, are in a sense trial pieces for his major life sequence, The *Cantos,* which he had begun even then. Both are attempts at sustained works made up of smaller units. The *Homage* is a single poem made of twelve loose translations or renderings of poems by Propertius, each of which had stood alone in the original. The effect, in Pound, is a series of more or less autonomous pieces that have an affinity for one another, a common language or flavor, a function in part of the latinate diction the poet employs. His *Mauberley* is a more recognizable sequence, since it has a character as its ostensible subject rather than the work of a poet. While the sections do add up to a whole, they are capable of standing alone, which over the years has come as a great relief to anthologists who have wished to recognize the poem's importance without allotting it full space. "Envoi (1919)" often appears singly, as do "Mauberley" and "Medallion." When read as a whole, and this may be where *Mauberley* is more of a true sequence than the *Homage*, the poems take on much greater meaning through the collective resonance. The renderings from Propertius are loosely affiliated, are similar to one another; the poems in *Mauberley* are parts of a whole.

It is in the *Cantos*, of course, that Pound works most concertedly in the poem sequence. Taking Dante's *Divine Comedy* as its extremely loose model (Pound once said he was writing a *commedia agnostica*), the poem works its way through ancient and modern history, Eastern and Western thought and art, economics, literature, politics, music, architecture, and personal experience. The array of sources and languages is dazzling, the obscurity of both sources and treatments daunting, the juxtapositions and leaps puzzling, and the effect maddening and delightful. The *Cantos* are a record of a modern poet's experience, an epic-scale work of the man of sensibility in the world. They are also a full-scale sequence in both depth and scope lacking in the poet's earlier work.

The unity of the sequence is established through purely internal means: echoes, repetitions, thematic and ideological ties. Pound's thought is of such a consistency that it can be nearly impossible to penetrate sometimes by a cursory encounter of a single poem. The apparent obscurity often is not so much a deliberate attempt to befuddle the reader or to allude to obscure materials as it is a function of the unity of the poet's mind; the obscure utterance will likely be expanded, explained, revised, rearticulated at some later point in the proceedings. The *Cantos*, as Allen Tate and others have noted, have a hermetic quality about them that can make reading a single canto difficult while rewarding a comprehensive reading of the whole. The publication history suggests that the *Cantos* can be read singly or in groups, coming out as they did by fits and starts over fifty years, but they prove most revealing when taken as a total work, when read as the epic they were intended to be. They are the ur-sequence of modern poetry. Tate says of them that they beg for a ceaseless study at the rate of one a year in depth, the whole to be read through every few weeks to recapture the flavor and maintain perspective.[14] His comments (which were made when there were only thirty *Cantos*) are suggestive of the demands modern literature makes upon its critics; works such as *Ulysses* and the *Cantos* are pitched away from the popular audience and toward the professional reader who can give them the kind of constant and loving attention they demand.

Throughout their entire length, the *Cantos* display Pound's indebtedness to his Imagist roots. They move by sudden leaps, relying always to a great degree on the moment, the image, the poet's ability to perceive and convey the brilliant instant, so that we are constantly being awakened by such lines as "the sun as a golden eye / between dark cloud and the mountain."[15] That sudden, sharp comparison is very much in the vein of "In a Station of the Metro" in its compression, clarity, and abruptness. Needless to say, such reliance on the brief image cannot in and of itself sustain a lengthy work, and the *Cantos* rely on radical juxtaposition as the main vehicle of movement. In this same Canto LXXXIII, for instance, he offers a paean to a dryad whose "eyes are like clouds." Four lines later, he expands on that comparison, so that the clouds are "over Taishan / When some of the rain has fallen / and half remains yet to fall." The refinement sharpens the image, giving it depth and solidity. What is most striking, however, are those four intervening lines between the image and its refinement:

> Nor can who has passed a month in the death cells
>   believe in capital punishment
> No man who has passed a month in the death cells
>   believes in cages for beasts.[16]

In the midst of this beautiful love-address, personal and political reality rears its head and requires the poet's attention. In this regard, the passage may be a model for the method of the *Cantos* as a whole: the aesthetic, the historical, the personal, the mythological, the political, and the spiritual—all exist side by side, separate, distinct, autonomous. Because of the poem's imagist tendencies, individual moments exist as self-contained scenes, instants, epiphanies. Competing or coexisting elements, then, do not so much interact as abut; their contrast is often startling, although it indicates not isolation but independence. These elements are all present; they are all identifiable as themselves; and their ragged relationships to one another follow their imperfect integration in the poet's life, in our own lives, in the world. Pound's interests are so wide ranging, his concerns so catholic, his sources and methods so far flung, that the technique of radical juxtaposition he carries with him from his Imagist days provides what may have been the only satisfactory method of composition.

At about the time the first thirty *Cantos* were appearing, another sequence was being written, this one a refutation of the wanderlust and classicism of Pound's work and of the wasteland mentality of Eliot's. *The Bridge* is Hart Crane's major work, without which he would in all likelihood be quite forgotten. It is a sequence much closer to Whitman than Pound, celebrating America and the American people, very much a homegrown thing. Where Pound is something of a literary Ulysses, traveling the known world for his materials, Crane relies on native sources, native speech, native treatments. Like most poets of his time, he had wrestled with the influence of Eliot and the Symbolists, learning much from them but being unwilling to remain in that camp. He found his liberation through Whitman, whose buoyant optimism and sense of universal connectedness countered Eliot's pessimism and exhaustion.

The result of that influence is impressive: if Eliot can connect nothing with nothing, then *The Bridge*, with its emphasis on connections, is the antithesis of Eliotic aesthetics. Crane finds connections everywhere, and the poem's two major symbols, the bridge (and tunnel as its inverse image) and the

river, both are connectors, uniting distant or separate elements of the country. They are a brilliant pair of symbols,
necessary complements. While the river connects one end of
the country with another, it also divides it and requires a
countersymbol; the bridge, ridiculous without a river under-
neath, provides the literally overarching image of unification.
The poem also strives to unify its disparate elements in ways
that neither Eliot's nor Pound's work needs to. The individual
poems in *The Bridge* are much more genuinely separate than
the individual cantos, certainly than the sections of *The Waste
Land*. For the most part, they are fully capable of standing
alone, poems of unquestionable autonomy. What they lack,
when separated from the whole, is the thematic power of his
emphasis on unity and wholeness. The constant harping on
the theme drives it home for the reader, the continual trans-
formations of the quotidian into the symbolic, the universal.
A bridge in New York becomes the symbol of America; a river
becomes the Mississippi, which becomes in turn another
symbol of the enormous variety and range of experience in
the country; a woman becomes Pocahontas, whose presence
in the poem leads toward an exploration of American history.
Crane shares with his contemporaries Sandburg and Dos
Passos a desire to write works that encompass the whole of
the American experience, that remain open to what the country has to offer, that embrace rather than reject.

Indeed, that very expansiveness sometimes gets him into
trouble with critics who, like Rosenthal and Gall, desire a
more intimate poetry:

> Crane, however, does not discover American life and memo-
> ries as Williams does. His sequence is not saturated with the
> intimately local sense of an experientially absorbed past that
> is one of *Paterson*'s triumphs. His use of American history and
> locales is more mechanically programmatic and rhetorical than
> Williams', and so is his use of our myths and "fabulae."[17]

While there is a great deal of accuracy about Crane's methods
and intentions in this criticism, there also is an element of
chiding the apple for not being a pear. Crane sets about to

use the public elements of American history, those aspects readily available to everyone, so the criticism that its history is that of the school text hardly comes as news. Crane paints, like Whitman, with broad strokes, trying to evoke the large scene; like Whitman, he attempts to be rhetorical, even mechanical; he seeks to capture America all at once.

Two poets of roughly the same generation have also worked on capturing America in their sequences, but they have differed from Crane's method in their insistence on the local as the key to the universal. Both *Paterson* and Charles Olson's *The Maximus Poems* portray American life by concentrating on individual cities. Neither work shows the kind of boundless enthusiasm that Crane displays, probably because their very close relationships to Paterson, New Jersey, and Gloucester, Massachusetts, force them to see society with its warts. Crane's general view, like Whitman's before him, affords him the luxury of not seeing the country close up, of blithely ignoring what does not suit him. Williams, on the other hand, can see all the squalor and pollution of the Passaic River and show them to the reader, but he can also see the falls. His optimism is a greater achievement than Crane's because harder won. So, too, with Olson, who even while railing against the economic exploitation of nature and what he calls the "perjoracracy" of American society can still see its possibilities.

While the two works share many similarities, they also are different in many ways. Each shows the preoccupations of its maker. *Paterson* reflects Williams' scientific interest in minutiae, his Imagist background, his passionate attachment to place. The poem focuses almost entirely on the city of Paterson and environs, scarcely bothering to suggest the ways it may be representative of larger society. That connection Williams leaves to the reader. He says repeatedly, "No ideas but in things," and he holds fast to that precept. He works through events, newspaper accounts, essays, personal recollection, and direct observation. One of the poem's great innovations, in fact, is its use of unreworked materials, such as newspaper reports, personal letters, historical accounts, in the poem itself. *Paterson* proceeds not by wrenching its materials into poetic form, but by building the poetry around the materials that are evidence of life; it is a genuinely organic work in the most exact sense of its growing out of, and thereby taking its form from, the sources it employs. Williams criticizes Eliot for the elitism of his poetry and his criticism, and in this work as in others he shows his own commitment to an egalitarian poetry through his openness. Unlike Eliot, he does not shy away from the contingency and chaos of life, does not feel obligated to superimpose an artificial order, but instead is content to live with what order he can discover in the world around him. He is closer to Crane and Whitman than to the method of the *Cantos*.

It is Olson who employs Pound's poetics toward an American poem. Like *Paterson*, *The Maximus Poems* are grounded in a specific place, but unlike it, they employ the sweeping style, the cross-cultural borrowing, the often declamatory tone of the *Cantos*. Tate says of Pound's work that, despite all the allusions, quotations, and foreign sources, the structure and method of the *Cantos* is simply conversational, the talk of literate men over a wide range of subjects. *The Maximus Poems* are also heavily conversational, relying on a listener for all the speaker's pronouncements. They embody a curious paradox: despite their ostensible epistolary structure (Olson calls the separate poems letters and even addresses some of them to various individuals), their principal unit is speech-related. These poems are the major work exemplifying Olson's theory of projective verse. In an attempt to break the tyranny of the traditional poetic line and the iambic foot, Olson proposes a system of "composition by field," of thinking in terms larger than the line, of composing by means not of a formal unit, but a logical one. The line of poetry should reflect the thought it contains and be limited by the breath of the speaker. A line, therefore, is roughly equivalent to an utterance and should be controlled by it, rather than forcing the thought to conform to the limitations of the line, as in traditional verse. His statements on the line as a "breath unit" are not entirely convincing, and few of the other practitioners of projective verse—Robert Duncan, Robert Creeley, Denise Levertov, Edward Dorn—have insisted on it as an essential part of the definition of what they do. Still, Olson does insist on the breath unit as the standard for the poetic line, and the result in *The Maximus Poems* is that the letters have a strikingly oral quality. What he is getting at with the breath unit is that each poet must strike his own rhythm, that poetry must be as personal as signature.

And indeed, Olson's poetic voice is intensely his own, as for that matter is Williams'. *The Maximus Poems* are strong, declamatory, aggressive as in this passage from Letter 5:

> the shocking play you publish
> with God as the Master of
> a Ship! In Gloucester-town
> you publish it, where men
> have cause to know where god is
> when wooden ships or steel ships,
> with sail or power,
> are out on men's business
> on waters which are tides, Ferrini,
> are not gods[18]

While Williams can also be didactic, even preachy, his more common moods in *Paterson* are softer, elegiac, meditative, conversational:

> We sit and talk and the
> silence speaks of the giants
> who have died in the past and have
> returned to those scenes unsatisfied
> and who is not unsatisfied, the
> silent, Singac the rock-shoulder
> emerging from the rocks—and the giants
> live again in your silence and
> unacknowledged desire—[19]

Williams is talking to someone in this passage; Olson is shouting at Ferrini in his. In each case, the poet must find the tone, the diction, the phrasing, the rhythm appropriate to his sensibility and his purpose *at each moment* of the poem. Unlike the traditional poet, twentieth-century writers cannot simply fall into a stride dictated at the outset by the metrical choices they make. Rather, they must make those choices constantly; their disjunctive poetics put a new emphasis on each line, each image, each passage. '

The history of modern poetry has been a history of finding, in Wallace Stevens' phrase, "what will suffice."[20] The poem from which it comes is called, significantly, "Of Modern Poetry," and Stevens outlines the problems for the modern writer: the world has changed; we live with wars of our own; new relationships between the sexes are taking place; our understanding of the workings of our own minds has changed and is changing. Given all that, how can poetry remain where it was, or what it was? The answer, obviously, is that it cannot, that it changes to meet the new requirements placed on it, the new environment in which it finds itself. The poetics of disjuncture generally, and the poem sequence in particular, have appealed and will continue to appeal to poets in this century because they allow the poet to work his way through the problems of being a poet in the modern world, of aspiring to epic scope, to the Godlike activity of creating worlds, while remaining on a profoundly human level.

7 / Conclusion

The oldest question in literary theory is the one about how society and literature fit together. Plato saw a split between their purposes and methods, and in a sense, the whole of critical history has been an attempt to answer his charges, to prove that poets should not be thrown out of the republic. The issue of the poet in society continues to be problematic in our time. Literature as a social act has been largely ignored in this century, in part because it was worded badly or discussed in the wrong terms, when it was considered at all. Only a handful of critics have seriously contemplated literature as literature (rather than as social artifact) within its social or historical context. But we must if literature is to have any further value for our culture. We live in an increasingly technological society that, more and more, sees the humanistic disciplines as irrelevant, even dilettantish. This view is supported by claims for poetic autonomy and art for art's sake. As a counter to this prevailing attitude toward literature, a more or less Platonic notion of the inferiority of poetry to nature or life, we must offer a more Aristotelian concept of literature, as the articulation of the whole of human experience.

In the realm of Modernist literature, there generally has been a separation of social-critical novels, plays, and poems from "art" works. We should move toward an understanding that every work presents a critique of or response to its society and history through its art; not just *Babbitt* and *McTeague* and *The Spoon River Anthology,* but *Ulysses* and *Four Quartets* and the *Cantos.* Such an understanding requires a great deal from the critic. Of course, no essay can accomplish everything at once; in the four critical essays in this study, a great many thoughts and insights had to be sacrificed to the pursuit of a central concept. Many of the ideas they put forth can be developed much further. They are intended not so much as models or suggestions as general directions in which to move, as attempts to articulate a way of reading literature.

That way has to do with nothing so much as expanding the notions of form and content so that they overlap and become indistinguishable. Our current notions of those two elements too often remain inside the work and simply reinforce the separation of society and literature by their narrowness. Let us replace them with notions that move outside the work. The act of creation is the process of giving shape and voice to a response to the world one finds; it is a social as well as a symbolic act. To consider form under such a concept as a purely internal matter, an ingenious device, is to falsify not only the nature of writing literature but the nature of reading it as well.

The reader is as much a part of the process of creation as is the writer. Were the reader merely passive, all criticism would look the same, everyone would find the same truths, the same techniques, and in a few months or years, critics would have said everything possible to say about the work. But controversy reigns in criticism, and *Hamlet* is as much a source of argument now as it has ever been. The reader's perspective on the work is different from the writer's, and the one may find ways the work relates to its history or previous literature or philosophy that the other never really thought about in the act of creation. The encounter is not one of produce-consumer but of cocreators in a dynamic exchange.

Modern literature presents a particularly vivid example of that exchange: the ways in which we read Modern works have undergone a transformation since its apparent demise and the rise of the Postmodern. This transformation is due in large measure to the reaction against Modernist sensibility among the post-World War I writers, as well as to the changes our world underwent in that war and the years since. Modern literature no longer shocks or befuddles us in quite the way it did when it was new, and yet it presents a series of problems to be worked out. That there is a Postmodernism colors the understanding of Modernism. Each new work, as Eliot said, changes the entire order, however slightly. Recent history has also changed some of our understandings of Modern works. Some of Lawrence and Kipling and Wyndham Lewis looks different after the Holocaust and the Civil Rights movement. But these are extreme examples. Every work changes, if only slightly, with the passing of time. Language changes, techniques become outmoded or accepted, styles give way to new styles. The reasons for these changes are complex.

The Modern writer is obsessed with form because the forms he finds left to him from earlier literature are not adequate to the task of interpreting the world he lives in. Similarly, the Postmodern writer rejects much that is characteristic of the Modern because the world has changed, and literature must as well. Art is neither tribeless nor timeless, as the young Yeats thought, and if we are to understand it fully, we must set about the chore of seeing it as intricately related to its people, its history, and its culture, as the articulation of the whole of human experience.

Notes

Modernism, Criticism, and the Social Dimension of Literature

[1]William A. Johnsen, "Toward a Redefinition of Modernism," *Boundary 2*, II, No. 3, (1974), 539.

[2]Monroe K. Spears, *Dionysus and the City* (New York: Oxford Univ. Press, 1971), pp. 12–15.

[3]Cyril Connolly, *The Modern Movement* (London: Hamisch Hamilton/Adre Duetsch, 1965), p. 2.

[4]William H. Gass, *Habitations of the Word* (New York: Simon and Schuster, 1985), p. 156.

[5]Maurice Beebe, "What Modernism Was," *Journal of Modern Literature*, III (July 1974), 1073.

[6]Edmund Wilson, *Axel's Castle* (New York: Scribner's, 1969 [1931]). Wilson's premise throughout the study is that the Modern writer follows the Symbolists in his pursuit of isolation and his rejection of political or social commitment.

[7]Connolly, p. 1.

[8]Robert Langbaum, *The Modern Spirit* (New York: Oxford Univ. Press, 1970), p. 183.

[9]Raymond Williams, *Modern Tragedy* (Stanford: Stanford Univ. Press, 1966). The specific arguments Williams puts forth regarding the failure of Modernism to produce great tragedy will be taken up later in the chapter.

[10]Langbaum, p. 177.

[11]Friedrich Nietzsche, *The Birth of Tragedy from the Spirit of Music,* and *The Case of Wagner,* trans. Walter Kaufmann (New York: Vintage, 1967).

[12]Spears, p. 44.

[13]Georg Lukács, *Realism in our Time,* trans. John Mander and Necke Mander, ed. George Steiner (New York: Harper and Row, 1971); at any number of points in the book; see especially the section "Franz Kafka or Thomas Mann." More specific arguments will be taken up later in the chapter.

[14]Beebe, p. 1074.

[15]I am aware of the irony of speaking of Modernism and attacking labels in the same paragraph. It will be fairly obvious by now, I think, that I am using *Modern* and *Modernist* more or less interchangeably and that I am referring to the time the writing took place as much as anything else.

[16]Graham Hough, *Image and Experience* (Lincoln: Univ. of Nebraska Press, 1960), p. 56.

[17]Harold Bloom, *The Anxiety of Influence* (New York: Oxford Univ. Press, 1973), p. 99.

[18]Ihab Hassan, *Paracriticisms: Seven Speculations of the Times* (Urbana: Univ. of Illinois Press, 1975), p. 52.

[19]Hassan, pp. 85–87.

[20]Jerome Klinowitz, *The Self-Apparent Word: Fiction as Language/ Language as Fiction* Carbondale: So. Illinois Univ. Press, 1984), p. 41.

[21]Michael Levenson, *A Geneaology of Modernism: A Study of English Literary Doctrine 1908–1922* (Cambridge: Cambridge Univ. Press, 1984), p. 79.

[22]Levenson, pp. 132–133.

[23]Spears, pp. 61–63.

[24]Johnsen pp. 544–545.

[25]T. S. Eliot, "Tradition and the Individual Talent," in *Selected Essays* (New York: Harcourt, Brace, 1950), p. 5.

[26]John Crowe Ransom, *The New Criticism* (Norfolk, Conn.: New Directions, 1941), p. 213.

[27]Ransom, p. xi.

[28]Yvor Winters, "The Anatomy of Nonsense," in *In Defense of Reason* (New York: Swallow Press, 1947), pp. 556 ff: and Allen Tate, "Miss Emily and the Bibliographer," in *Essays of Four Decades* (Chicago: Swallow Press, 1968), pp. 141 ff.

[29]Cleanth Brooks, *The Well Wrought Urn* (New York: Harcourt, Brace, 1947), p. 215. Subsequent references to this edition will be included in the text in parenthesis as, in this case, (Urn, 215).

³⁰Kenneth Burke, *Language as Symbolic Action* (Berkeley: Univ. of California Press, 1966), pp. 481 ff., esp. 496–506.

³¹Brooks; see especially his discussion of Wordsworth's "Ode: Intimations of Immortality."

³²Winters, *The Function of Criticism* (Denver: Swallow Press, 1957), p. 16.

³³Ransom, especially pp. 212–234.

³⁴Tate, "Modern Poetry," in *Essays of Four Decades*, p. 212.

³⁵Northrop Frye, *Anatomy of Criticism* (Princeton: Princeton Univ. Press, 1957), p. 18. Subsequent references to this edition will be included in the text in parenthesis as, for example, (AC, 18).

³⁶Harold Bloom, *The Anxiety of Influence*, p. 99. Subsequent references will be included in the text in parenthesis as, for example, (AI, 99).

³⁷Northrop Frye, *Fables of Identity* (New York: Harcourt, Brace, 1963), p. 21. Subsequent references will be included in the text in parenthesis as, for example, (FI, 21).

³⁸Wallace Stevens, *Collected Poems* (New York: Knopf, 1977) pp. 202, 239.

³⁹Fredric Jameson, *The Prison-House of Language*, (Princeton: Princeton Univ. Press, 1972), pp. 195–196. Subsequent references will be included in the text in parenthesis as, in this case, (P-H, 195–196).

⁴⁰Fredric Jameson, *Marxism and Form* (Princeton: Princeton Univ. Press, 1971), p. 307. Subsequent references will be included in the text in parenthesis as, in this case, (M&F, 307).

⁴¹Lukács, p. 70. Subsequent references to this edition will be included in the text in parenthesis as, for example, (RT, 70).

⁴²Raymond Williams, *Modern Tragedy* (Stanford: Stanford Univ. Press, 1966), p. 54. Subsequent references will be included in the text in parentheses as, in this case, (MT, 54).

⁴³Jonathan Culler, *On Deconstruction* (Ithaca: Cornell Univ. Press, 1982), p. 219. Subsequent references will be included in the text in parentheses as, in this case, (OD, 219).

⁴⁴Barbara Johnson, *The Critical Difference* (Baltimore: Johns Hopkins Univ. Press, 1980), p. 5.

⁴⁵Jacques Derrida, *Positions* (Chicago: Univ. of Chicago Press, 1981), pp. 38–39/27, as cited by Culler.

⁴⁶Harold Bloom, *Agon* (New York: Oxford Univ. Press, 1982) pp. 335–336.

⁴⁷See, for instance, Frank Lentricchia, *After the New Criticism* (London: Methuen, 1980), p. 169.

[48]Bloom, p. 37

[49]Shoshana Felman, "Turning the Screw of Interpretation," *Yale French Studies* 55/56 (1977), p. 201.

The Waste Land and the Great War

[1]Eliot, pp. 4–5.

[2]Wilson, p. 121.

[3]Eliot, *Complete Poems and Plays* (New York: Harcourt, Brace, 1971), p. 50. All subsequent references to Eliot's poetry will be to this edition, and will be accompanied by line references in parenthesis in the text.

[4]Northrop Frye, *T. S. Eliot* (London: Oliver and Boyd, 1963), p. 52.

[5]Frye, *Anatomy*, pp. 20–25. Frye's use of commodity structure as the metaphor for the writer–reader–text–critic relationship could not be less happy, although it is a apt metaphor for the sort of "freezing" of the literary work that he proposes.

[6]Harriet Davidson, *T. S. Eliot and Hermeneutics: Absence and Interpretation in* The Waste Land. (Baton Rouge: Louisiana State University Press, 1985), p. 326.

[7]Paul Fussell, *The Great War and Modern Memory* (New York: Oxford Univ. Press, 1975), p. 326.

[8]Robert Sencourt, *T. S. Eliot: A Memoir* (New York: Dodd, Mead, 1971), p. 65.

[9]Anne Wright, *Literature of Crisis, 1910–1922* (London: Macmillan, 1984), pp. 170–171.

[10]Frye, *T. S. Eliot*, p. 62.

[11]Frye, *T. S. Eliot*, p. 49.

[12]See, for instance, Robert Parkinson, *The Origins of World War One* (New York: Putnam's, 1970), on the subject of the relationship between economics, imperialism, and the oncoming of the Great War.

[13]Eloise Knapp Hay, *T. S. Eliot's Negative Way* (Cambridge: Harvard Univ. Press, 1982), p. 49.

[14]Fussell, p. 239.

[15]Fussell, p. 301.

[16]Hugh Kenner, *The Invisible Poet: T. S. Eliot* (New York: Harcourt, 1959), p. 160.

[17]Hay, p. 67.

[18]Kenner, pp. 193–194.

Go Down, Moses, History, and Narrative Form

[1]Jean-Paul Sartre, "On *The Sound and the Fury:* Time in the Novels of William Faulkner," in *Faulkner,* ed. Robert Penn Warren (Englewood Cliffs, N. J.: Prentice-Hall, 1966). Sartre's argument with *The Sound and the Fury,* true also of a number of Faulkner's novels, that it has a past but no future, can be satisfied in *Go Down, Moses,* for however much it seems to dwell in the past, it is going somewhere.

[2]Thadious M. Davis, *Faulkner's "Negro": Art and the Southern Context* (Baton Rouge: Louisiana State Univ. Press, 1983), p. 243.

[3]Davis, p. 239.

[4]Malcolm Cowley, "Go Down to Faulkner's Land," *New Republic* (29 June 1942), p. 900.

[5]William Faulkner, *Go Down, Moses* (New York: Vintage, 1973), p. 3. Subsequent references to pages in this edition appear in the text following the quoted material.

[6]Carl Rollyson, *Uses of the Past in the Novels of William Faulkner* (Ann Arbor, Mich.: UMI Research Press, 1984), pp. 102–103.

[7]John Pilkington, *The Heart of Yoknapatawpha* (Jackson: Univ. of Mississippi Press, 1981), p. 247.

[8]A comparison of the uses of games of chance in *Go Down, Moses,* in which the emphasis is shifted away from the cosmic toward the human, and other works, particularly *The Sound and the Fury,* might prove enlightening.

[9]Joseph Blotner, ed., *Selected Letters of William Faulkner* (New York: Vintage, 1978), p. 185.

[10]Warren Beck, *Faulkner* (Madison: Univ. of Wisconsin Press, 1976), p. 346.

[11]Blotner, pp. 175–176.

[12]E. M. Forster, *A Passage to India* (New York: Harcourt, Brace, 1952), p. 322.

[13]Edmond Volpe, *A Reader's Guide to William Faulkner* (New York: Farrar, Straus, 1964), p. 231.

[14]Pilkington, p. 287.

Ulysses and Joyce's Grammar of Social Experience

[1]From Wilson's *Axel's Castle* on, this has been a sort of minor critical convention in discussions of *Ulysses.*

[2]Stanley Sultan, *The Argument of* Ulysses (Columbus: Ohio State Univ. Press, 1964).

[3]Hugh Kenner, *Joyce's Voices* (Berkeley: Univ. of California Press,

1978). Kenner maintains that throughout his career Joyce is a nasty eavesdropper in his role as narrator.

[4]The critics are not simply imagining the concept of superimposed order from out of nowhere. Joyce started the whole problem when he handed out copies of the Schema when the novel first came out.

[5]See, for instance, Mary Parr, *James Joyce: The Poetry of Conscience* (Milwaukee: Inland. Press, 1961), and John Garvin, *James Joyce's Disunited Kingdom and the Irish Dimension* (New York: Barnes and Noble, 1976), as two examples of overzealous pursuit of biographical information.

[6]Wilson, p. 214.

[7]Stanley Sultan, Ulysses, The Waste Land, *and Modernism* (Port Washington, N. Y.: Kennikat Press, 1977), p. 49.

[8]Lukács, p. 18.

[9]Lukács, p. 21.

[10]Lukács, p. 21.

[11]James Joyce, *Ulysses* (New York: Random House, 1961), p. 658). Subsequent references will be included in the text in parenthesis as, in this case, (U, 658).

[12]Kenner, p. 69.

[13]Joyce, *Critical Writings,* ed. Ellsworth Mason and Richard Ellmann (New York: Viking, 1973), p. 171. Subsequent references will be included in the text in parenthesis as, in this case, (CW, 171).

[14]Stuart Gilbert, *James Joyce's* Ulysses (New York: Vintage, 1955), p. 177.

[15]Suzette Henke, *Joyce's Moraculous Sindbook* (Columbus: Ohio State Univ. Press, 1978), p. 250.

Yeats's Middle Poetry and the Politics of Vision

[1]William Butler Yeats, *Essays and Introductions* (New York: Collier, 1973), p. 522.

[2]Yeats, *The Collected Poems of William Butler Yeats* (New York: Macmillan, 1951), p. 39. Subsequent references to this edition will be included in the text in parenthesis as, in this case, (CP, 39).

[3]Frye, *Fables,* p. 222.

[4]Wilson, p. 46.

[5]Thomas Parkinson, "Yeats and the Limits of Modernity," *Yeats: An Annual of Critical and Textual Studies* III, eds. George Bornstein and Richard J. Finneran. (Ithaca: Cornell Univ. Press, 1985), p. 68.

[6]Debra Journet, "Yeats's Quarrel with Modernism," *Southern Review,* 20, No. 1 (1984), pp. 41–45.

[7]Richard Ellmann, *The Identity of Yeats* (New York: Oxford Univ. Press, 1964), p. 153.

[8]Yeats, *A Vision* (New York: Collier, 1973 [1937]), p. 266.

[9]Louis MacNeice, *The Poetry of W. B. Yeats* (New York: Oxford Univ. Press, 1969 [1941]), p. 193.

[10]Ellmann, p. 200.

[11]Ellmann, *Yeats: The Man and the Masks* (New York: Dutton, 1958), pp. 244–245.

[12]MacNiece, p. 129.

[13]Arra M. Garab, *Beyond Byzantium: The Last Phase of Yeats's Career* (DeKalb: Northern Illinois Univ. Press, 1969), p. 3.

[14]Ellmann, *Identity,* p. 285.

[15]Edmund Wilson is an early and vocal proponent of such a view, but by no means the only one.

So Much Depends

[1]Virginia Woolf, *Mrs. Dalloway* (New York: Harcourt, 1953), p. 31.

[2]Geoffrey Bullough, *The Trend of Modern Poetry* (Edinburgh: Oliver and Boyd, 1934), pp. 46–77.

[3]Bullough, pp. 113–120.

[4]Ezra Pound, *Literary Essays of Ezra Pound* (New York: New Directions, 1968), p. 3.

[5]William Pratt, *The Imagist Poem* (New York: Dutton, 1963), p. 14. For a more extended discussion of Imagist theories, see John T. Gage, *In the Arresting Eye: The Rhetoric of Imagism* (Baton Rouge: Louisiana State Univ. Press, 1981), esp. pp. 1–31.

[6]Pound, p. 4.

[7]Pound, *Selected Poems of Ezra Pound* (New York: New Directions, 1957), p. 35.

[8]H. D., *Collected Poems 1912–1944* (New York: New Directions, 1983), p. 55.

[9]Arthur Symons, *Dramatis Personae* (Indianapolis: Bobbs, Merrill, 1923), p. 107.

[10]Hugh Kenner, *The Pound Era* (Berkeley: Univ. of California Press, 1971), pp. 486–488. Kenner points out Pound making peace with Whitman through echoes of his work in Canto 82.

[11]Linda W. Wagner, *American Modern* (Port Washington, N. Y.: Kennikat, 1980), pp. 22–23.

[12]Stan Smith, *Inviolable Voice: History and Twentieth-Century Poetry* (Dublin: Gill and Macmillan, 1982), p. 9.

[13]M. L. Rosenthal and Sally M. Gall, *The Modern Poetic Sequence: The Genius of Modern Poetry* (New York: Oxford Univ. Press, 1983), p. 9.

[14]Allen Tate, *Essays of Four Decades* (Chicago: Swallow, 1968), p. 371.

[15]Ezra Pound, *The Cantos of Ezra Pound* (New York: New Directions, 1975), p. 531.

[16]Pound, *Cantos*, p. 530.

[17]Rosenthal and Gall, p. 316.

[18]Charles Olson, *The Maximus Poems* (New York: Jargon/Corinth, 1960), p. 25.

[19]William Carlos Williams, *Paterson* (New York: New Directions, 1963), p. 25.

[20]Wallace Stevens, *Collected Poems* (New York: Knopf, 1977), p. 239.

Bibliography

Adams, Robert Martin. *Surface and Symbol: The Consistency of James Joyce's* Ulysses. New York: Oxford Univ. Press, 1962.

———. *After Joyce: Studies in Fiction after* Ulysses. New York: Oxford Univ. Press, 1977.

Beck, Warren. *Faulkner.* Madison: Univ. of Wisconsin Press, 1976.

Beebe, Maurice. "*Ulysses* and the Age of Modernism." *James Joyce Quarterly,* 10 (1972), 172–188.

———. "What Modernism Was." *Journal of Modern Literature,* 3 (July 1974), 1065–1084.

Beja, Morris. *Epiphany in the Modern Novel.* Seattle: Univ. of Washington Press, 1971.

———, ed. *James Joyce,* Dubliners, *and* A Portrait of the Artist as a Young Man: *A Selection of Critical Essays.* London: Macmillan, 1973.

Benstock, Bernard. *James Joyce: The Undiscovered Country.* New York: Barnes and Noble, 1977.

Bergonzi, Bernard, ed. *The Twentieth Century.* London: Barrie and Jenkins, 1970.

———. *The Myth of Modernism and Twentieth Century Literature.* Brighton, Sussex: Harvester, 1986.

Blackmur, R. P. *Anni Mirabiles 1921–1925: Reason in the Madness of Letters.* Washington, D.C.: Library of Congress, 1956.

———. *Form and Value in Modern Literature.* Garden City, N. Y.: Doubleday, 1957.

Bloom, Harold. *The Anxiety of Influence.* New York: Oxford Univ. Press, 1973.

————. *Agon: Towards a Theory of Revisionism.* New York: Oxford Univ. Press, 1982.

————. *The Breaking of the Vessels.* Chicago: Univ. of Chicago Press, 1982.

Blotner, Joseph. *Faulkner: A Biography.* New York: Random House, 1974.

————, ed. *Selected Letters of William Faulkner.* New York: Vintage, 1977.

Bolgan, Anne C. *What the Thunder Really Said.* Montreal: McGill-Queen's Univ. Press, 1973.

Bradbury, Malcolm. *The Social Context of Modern English Literature.* New York: Schocken, 1971.

————. *The Modern American Novel.* New York: Oxford Univ. Press, 1983.

————, and James McFarlane, eds. *Modernism 1890–1930.* New York: Penguin, 1976.

Brooks, Cleanth. *The Well Wrought Urn.* New York: Harcourt, Brace, 1947.

————. *William Faulkner: The Yoknapatawpha Country.* New Haven: Yale Univ. Press, 1963.

————. *Modern Poetry and the Tradition.* New York: Oxford Univ. Press, 1965.

————. *A Shaping Joy.* New York: Harcourt, Brace, 1947.

Budgen, Frank. *James Joyce and the Making of Ulysses.* London: Oxford Univ. Press, 1972.

Bullough, Geoffrey. *The Trend of Modern Poetry.* Edinburgh: Oliver and Boyd, 1934.

Burke, Kenneth. *Language as Symbolic Action.* Berkeley: Univ. of California Press, 1966.

Buttel, Robert. "The Incandescence of Old Age: Yeats and Stevens in Their Late Poems." *American Poetry Review,* Jan.–Feb. 1983, pp. 42–44.

Carothers, James B. *William Faulkner's Short Stories.* Ann Arbor, Mich.: UMI Research Press, 1985.

Chatterjee, Bhabatosh. *The Poetry of W. B. Yeats.* Calcutta: Orient Longmans, 1962.

Connolly, Cyril. *The Modern Movement.* London: Hamisch Hamilton/Andre Deutsch, 1965.

Creighton, Joanne V. *William Faulkner's Craft of Revision.* Detroit: Wayne State Univ. Press, 1977.

Culler, Jonathon. *Structuralist Poetics: Structuralism, Linguistics, and the Study of Literature*. Ithaca: Cornell Univ. Press, 1975.

———. *On Deconstruction: Theory and Criticism after Structuralism*. Ithaca: Cornell Univ. Press, 1982.

Daiches, David. *The Novel and the Modern World*. Chicago: Univ. of Chicago Press, 1960.

Davidson, Harriet. *T. S. Eliot and Hermeneutics: Absence and Interpretation in* The Waste Land. Baton Rouge: Louisiana State Univ. Press, 1985.

Davis, Thadious M. *Faulkner's "Negro": Art and the Southern Context*. Baton Rouge: Louisiana State Univ. Press, 1983.

De Man, Paul. *Blindness and Insight: Essays in the Rhetoric of Contemporary Criticism*. Minneapolis: Univ. of Minnesota Press, 1983.

Donnelly, Sheila Hurst. "Ike McCaslin: Fugitive from Responsibility, Poet of Cloistered Virtue." *Mid-Hudson Language Studies*, 7 (1984), 64–65.

D(oolittle), H(ilda). *Collected Poems 1912–1944*. Ed. Louis L. Martz. New York: New Directions, 1983.

Early, James. *The Making of* Go Down, Moses. Dallas: Southern Methodist Univ. Press, 1972.

Eco, Umberto. *The Aesthetics of Chaosmos: The Middle Ages of James Joyce*. Trans. Ellen Esrock. Tulsa: Univ. of Tulsa, 1982.

Ehrlich, Heyward, ed. *Light Rays: James Joyce and Modernism*. New York: New Horizon, 1984.

Eliot, T. S. *Selected Essays*. New York: Harcourt, Brace, 1950.

———. *Collected Poems and Plays*. New York: Harcourt, Brace, 1971.

Ellman, Richard. *Yeats: The Man and the Masks*. New York: Dutton, 1958.

———. *The Identity of Yeats*. New York: Oxford Univ. Press, 1964.

———. *Ulysses on the Liffey*. New York: Oxford Univ. Press, 1972.

———. *James Joyce*. New York: Oxford Univ. Press, 1974.

———. *Selected Joyce Letters*. New York: Viking, 1975.

Epstein, Edmund L., ed. *Work in Progress: Joyce Centenary Essays*. Carbondale: Southern Illinois Univ. Press, 1983.

Faulkner, Peter. *Modernism*. London: Methuen, 1977.

Faulkner, William. *The Sound and the Fury*. New York: Modern College Library, 1956.

———. *Light in August*. New York: Modern Library, 1959.

———. *Go Down, Moses*. New York: Vintage, 1973.

Felman, Shoshana. "Turning the Screw of Interpretation." *Yale French Studies*, 55/56 (1977) 94–202.

Flores, Ralph. *The Rhetoric of Doubtful Authority: Deconstructive Read-*

ings of Self-Questioning Narratives, St. Augustine to Faulkner. Ithaca: Cornell Univ. Press, 1984.

Forster, E. M. *A Passage to India.* New York: Harcourt, Brace, 1952.

Frye, Northrop. *Anatomy of Criticism.* Princeton: Princeton Univ. Press, 1957.

———. *Fables of Identity.* New York: Harcourt, Brace, 1963.

———. *T. S. Eliot.* London: Oliver and Boyd, 1963.

———. *The Educated Imagination.* Bloomington: Indiana Univ. Press, 1964.

Fussell, Paul. *The Great War and Modern Memory.* New York: Oxford Univ. Press, 1975.

Gage, John T. *In the Arresting Eye: The Rhetoric of Imagism.* Baton Rouge: Louisiana State Univ. Press, 1981.

Garab, Arra M. *Beyond Byzantium: The Last Phase of Yeats's Career.* DeKalb: Northern Illinois Univ. Press, 1969.

Garvin, John. *James Joyce's Disunited Kingdom and the Irish Dimension.* New York: Barnes and Noble, 1976.

Gass, William. *Fiction and the Figures of Life.* New York: Knopf, 1970.

———. *The World Within the Word.* New York: Knopf, 1978.

———. *Habitations of the Word.* New York: Simon and Schuster, 1985.

Gilbert, Stuart. *James Joyce's Ulysses.* New York: Vintage, 1955.

Goldman, Arnold. *The Joyce Paradox: Form and Freedom in His Fiction.* Evanston: Northwestern Univ. Press, 1966.

Goodheart, Eugene. *The Failure of Criticism.* Cambridge: Harvard Univ. Press, 1978.

Gottfried, Roy K. *The Art of Joyce's Syntax in* Ulysses. Athens: Univ. of Georgia Press, 1980.

Gunnar, Eugenia M. *T. S. Eliot's Romantic Dilemma: Tradition's Anti-Traditional Elements.* New York: Garland, 1985.

Harmon, Maurice, ed. *The Irish Writer and the City.* Totowa, N. J.: Barnes and Noble, 1984.

Hartman, Geoffrey H. *Beyond Formalism.* New Haven: Yale Univ. Press, 1970.

Hassan, Ihab. *The Dismemberment of Orpheus: Toward a Postmodern Literature.* New York: Oxford Univ. Press, 1971.

———. *Paracriticisms: Seven Speculations of the Times.* Urbana: Univ. of Illinois Press, 1975.

Hay, Eloise Knapp. *T. S. Eliot's Negative Way.* Cambridge: Harvard Univ. Press, 1982.

Hayman, David. Ulysses: *The Mechanics of Meaning.* Madison: Univ. of Wisconsin Press, 1982.

Henke, Suzette A. *Joyce's Moraculous Sindbook*. Columbus: Ohio State Univ. Press, 1978.

Henn, Thomas Rice. *The Lonely Tower: Studies in the Poetry of W. B. Yeats*. London: Methuen, 1965.

Herring, Philip F. "Joyce's Politics." In *New Light on Joyce*. Ed. Fritz Senn. Bloomington: Indiana Univ. Press, 1972.

Hirsch, E. D., Jr. *Validity in Interpretation*. New Haven: Yale Univ. Press, 1967.

Hone, Joseph. *W. B. Yeats, 1865–1939*. London: Macmillan, 1962.

Hough, Graham. *Image and Experience: Reflections on a Literary Revolution*. Lincoln: Univ. of Nebraska Press, 1960.

Houghton, Norris. *The Exploding Stage: An Introduction to Twentieth Century Drama*. New York: Weybright and Talley, 1971.

Irwin, John T. *Doubling and Incest/Revenge and Repetition: A Speculative Reading of Faulkner*. Baltimore: Johns Hopkins Univ. Press, 1975.

Jameson, Fredric. *Marxism and Form*. Princeton: Princeton Univ. Press, 1971.

———. *The Prison-House of Language*. Princeton: Princeton Univ. Press, 1972.

Jeffares, A. N. *The Circus Animals: Essays on W. B. Yeats*. London: Macmillan, 1970.

———. *W. B. Yeats*. London: Routledge and Kegan Paul, 1971.

Johnsen, William A. "Toward a Redefinition of Modernism." *Boundary 2*, II, No. 3 (1974), 539–556.

Johnson, Barbara. *The Critical Difference: Essays in the Contemporary Rhetoric of Reading*. Baltimore: Johns Hopkins Univ. Press, 1980.

Journet, Debra. "Yeats's Quarrel with Modernism." *Southern Review*, XX, No. 1 (1984), 41–53.

Joyce, James. *Ulysses*. New York: Random House, 1961.

———. *Dubliners*. New York: Modern Library, 1969.

———. *A Portrait of the Artist as a Young Man*. New York: Viking, 1971.

———. *The Critical Writings*. Eds. Ellsworth Mason and Richard Ellmann. New York: Viking, 1973.

Kenner, Hugh. *The Invisible Poet: T. S. Eliot*. New York: Harcourt, 1959.

———. *The Pound Era*. Berkeley: Univ. of California Press, 1971.

———. *A Homemade World*. New York: Knopf, 1975.

———. *Joyce's Voices*. Berkeley: Univ. of California Press, 1978.

Kermode, Frank. *The Sense of an Ending*. New York: Oxford Univ. Press, 1966.

Kerr, Elizabeth M. *William Faulkner's Gothic Domain.* Port Washington, N. Y.: Kennikat, 1979.

Kiely, Robert, and John Hildebrand, eds. *Modernism Reconsidered.* Cambridge: Harvard Univ. Press, 1983.

Kirk, Russell. *Eliot and His Age.* New York: Random House, 1971.

Klinkowitz, Jerome. *The Practice of Fiction in America: Writers from Hawthorne to the Present.* Ames: Univ. of Iowa Press, 1980.

————. *The Self-Apparent Word: Fiction as Language/Language as Fiction.* Carbondale: Southern Illinois Univ. Press, 1984.

Knoll, Robert E. *Storm over* The Waste Land. New York: Scott, Foresman, 1964.

Kojecky, Roger. *T. S. Eliot's Social Criticism.* London: Faber, 1971.

Kuyk, Dirk, Jr. *Threads Cable-Strong: William Faulkner's* Go Down, Moses. Lewisburg, Pa.: Bucknell Univ. Press, 1983.

Langbaum, Robert. *The Modern Spirit.* New York: Oxford Univ. Press, 1970.

Leavis, F. R. *New Bearings in English Poetry.* London: Chatto and Windus, 1932; rpt. London: Penguin, 1972.

Lentricchia, Frank. *After the New Criticism.* London: Methuen, 1980.

Levenson, Michael H. *A Genealogy of Modernism: A Study of English Literary Doctrine 1908–1922.* Cambridge: Cambridge Univ. Press, 1984.

Levin, Harry. *Refractions: Essays in Comparative Literature.* New York: Oxford Univ. Press, 1966.

Lewis, Philip. "The Post-Structuralist Condition." *Diacritics,* 12, No. 1 (1982), 1–24.

Litz, Walton. "Genealogy as Symbol in *Go Down, Moses.*" *Faulkner Studies,* I (1952), 49–53.

Lodge, David. *The Modes of Modern Writing: Metaphor, Metonymy, and the Typology of Modern Literature.* London: Edward Arnold, 1977.

Lukács, Georg. *Realism in Our Time.* Trans. John Mander and Necke Mander. New York: Harper, 1971.

————. *The Theory of the Novel.* Trans. Anna Bostock. Cambridge: MIT Press, 1971.

Macleish, Archibald. *A Time to Speak: The Selected Prose.* Boston: Houghton-Mifflin, 1941.

MacNeice, Louis. *The Poetry of W. B. Yeats.* New York: Oxford Univ. Press, 1969.

Malin, Irving. *William Faulkner: An Interpretation.* Stanford: Stanford Univ. Press, 1957.

Martin, Jay, ed. *A Collection of Critical Essays on* The Waste Land. Englewood Cliffs, N. J.: Prentice-Hall, 1968.

Matthiesson, F. O. *The Achievement of T. S. Eliot*. Boston: Houghton-Mifflin, 1935.

Maxwell, D. E. S. *The Poetry of T. S. Eliot*. London: Routledge and Kegan Paul, 1960.

McCormack, W. J., and Alistair Stead, eds. *James Joyce and Modern Literature*. London: Routledge and Kegan Paul, 1982.

Mellard, James M. *The Exploded Form: The Modernist Novel in America*. Urbana: Univ. of Illinois Press, 1980.

Millgate, Michael. *The Achievement of William Faulkner*. New York: Random House, 1966.

Minter, David. *William Faulkner: His Life and Work*. Baltimore: Johns Hopkins Univ. Press, 1980.

Mokashi-Punekar, Shankar. *The Later Phase in the Development of W. B. Yeats*. N.p.: Dharwar-Karnatak Univ. Press, 1966.

Olson, Charles. *The Maximus Poems*. New York: Jargon/Corinth, 1960.

Parkinson, Roger. *The Origins of World War One*. New York: Putnam's, 1970.

Parkinson, Thomas. *W. B. Yeats: The Later Poetry*. Berkeley: Univ. of California Press, 1966.

———. "Yeats and the Limits of Modernity." *Yeats: An Annual of Critical and Textual Studies*, Vol. III. Eds. George Bornstein and Richard J. Finneran. Ithaca: Cornell Univ. Press, 1985.

Parr, Mary. *James Joyce: The Poetry of Conscience*. Milwaukee: Inland Press, 1961.

Peake, C. H. *James Joyce: The Citizen and the Artist*. Stanford: Stanford Univ. Press, 1977.

Pearce, Richard. *The Novel in Motion: An Approach to Modern Fiction*. Columbus: Ohio State Univ. Press, 1983.

Peavy, Charles D. *Go Slow Now: Faulkner and the Race Question*. Eugene: Univ. of Oregon Press, 1971.

Pilkington, John. *The Heart of Yoknapatawpha*. Jackson: Univ. of Mississippi Press, 1981.

Pound, Ezra. *Selected Poems of Ezra Pound*. New York: New Directions, 1957.

———. *Literary Essays of Ezra Pound*. New York: New Directions, 1968.

———. *The Cantos of Ezra Pound*. New York: New Directions, 1975.

Pratt, William. *The Imagist Poem*. New York: Dutton, 1963.

Raban, Jonathan. *The Technique of Modern Fiction: Essays in Practical Criticism*. Notre Dame, Indiana: Notre Dame Univ. Press, 1969.

Raine, Kathleen. *Yeats, the Tarot, and the Golden Dawn*. Dublin: Dolmen, 1972.

Ransom, John Crowe. *The New Criticism*. Norfolk, Conn.: New Directions, 1941.

Riquelme, John Paul. *Teller and Tale in Joyce's Fiction: Oscillating Perspectives*. Baltimore: Johns Hopkins Univ. Press, 1983.

Rollyson, Carl E. *Uses of the Past in the Novels of William Faulkner*. Ann Arbor, Mich.: UMI Research Press, 1984.

Rosenthal, M. L. *The Modern Poets: A Critical Introduction*. New York: Oxford Univ. Press, 1960.

———, and Sally M. Gall. *The Modern Poetic Sequence: The Genius of Modern Poetry*. New York: Oxford Univ. Press, 1983.

Schneider, Elisabeth. *T. S. Eliot: The Pattern in the Carpet*. Berkeley: Univ. of California Press, 1975.

Schorer, Mark. *Modern British Fiction*. New York: Oxford Univ. Press, 1961.

Schricker, Gale C. *A New Species of Man: The Poetic Persona of W. B. Yeats*. Lewisburg, Pa.: Bucknell Univ. Press, 1982.

Sencourt, Robert. *T. S. Eliot, A Memoir*. New York: Dodd, Mead, 1971.

Smith, Stan. *Inviolable Voice: History and Twentieth-Century Poetry*. Dublin: Gill and Macmillan, 1982.

Spears, Monroe K. *Dionysus and the City*. New York: Oxford Univ. Press, 1971.

Spender, Stephen. *The Struggle of the Modern*. Berkeley: Univ. of California Press, 1963.

Staley, Thomas F. and Bernard Benstock. *Approaches to* Ulysses: *Ten Essays*. Pittsburgh: Univ. of Pittsburgh Press, 1970.

Stevens, Wallace. *The Necessary Angel*. New York: Vintage, 1951.

———. *Collected Poems*. New York: Knopf, 1977.

Sultan, Stanley. *The Argument of* Ulysses. Columbus: Ohio State Univ. Press, 1964.

———. Ulysses, The Waste Land, *and Modernism*. Port Washington, N. Y.: Kennikat Press, 1977.

Symons, Arthur. *Dramatis Personae*. Indianapolis: Bobbs, Merrill, 1923.

Tate, Allen. *T. S. Eliot: The Man and His Work*. New York: Delacorte, 1966.

———. *Essays of Four Decades*. Chicago: Swallow, 1968.

Thurley, Geoffrey. *The Ironic Harvest: English Poetry in the Twentieth Century*. London: Edward Arnold, 1974.

————. *The Turbulent Dream: Passion and Politics in the Poetry of W. B. Yeats*. Santa Lucia: Univ. of Queensland Press, 1983.

Thwaite, Anthony. *Twentieth-Century English Poetry*. New York: Barnes and Noble, 1978.

Tindall, William York. *James Joyce: His Way of Interpreting the Modern World*. New York: Scribner's, 1965.

Torchiana, Donald T. "Joyce and Dublin." In *The Irish Writer and the City*. Totowa, N. J.: Barnes and Noble, 1984, pp. 52–64.

Unger, Leonard. *T. S. Eliot: Moments and Patterns*. Minneapolis: Univ. of Minnesota Press, 1966.

Vendler, Helen H. *Yeats's* Vision *and the Later Plays*. Cambridge: Harvard Univ. Press, 1963.

Wagner, Linda W. *American Modern: Essays in Fiction and Poetry*. Port Washington, N. Y.: Kennikat, 1980.

Watkins, Evan. *The Critical Act: Criticism and Community*. New Haven: Yale Univ. Press, 1978.

Whitaker, Thomas Russell. *Swan and Shadow: Yeats's Dialogue with History*. Chapel Hill: Univ. of North Carolina Press, 1964.

Wilde, Alan. *Horizons of Assent: Modernism, Postmodernism, and the Ironic Imagination*. Baltimore: Johns Hopkins Univ. Press, 1981.

Williams, Raymond. *Modern Tragedy*. Stanford: Stanford Univ. Press, 1966.

Williams, William Carlos. *Paterson*. New York: New Directions, 1963.

Wilson, Edmund. *Axel's Castle: A Study in the Imaginative Literature of 1870–1930*. New York: Scribner's, 1969.

Wilson, F. A. C. *W. B. Yeats and Tradition*. London: Gollancz, 1958.

Winters, Yvor. *In Defense of Reason*. New York: Swallow and Wm. Morrow, 1947.

————. *The Function of Criticism: Problems and Exercises*. Denver: Swallow, 1957.

Woolf, Virginia. *Mrs. Dalloway*. New York: Harcourt, 1953.

————. *Granite and Rainbow*. London: Hogarth, 1960.

Wright, Anne. *Literature of Crisis, 1910–1922*. London: Macmillan, 1984.

Wright, George T. *The Poet in the Poem: The Personae of Eliot, Yeats, and Pound*. Berkeley: Univ. of California Press, 1960.

Yeats, William Butler. *The Collected Poems of William Butler Yeats*. New York: Macmillan, 1951.

————. *Essays and Introductions*. New York: Collier, 1973.

————. *A Vision*. New York: Collier, 1973.

Index